2017

Dear C...

In prep...
next t...

From your Aussie 'family'

xxxxxxxx

MOUNT BUGGERY TO NOWHERE ELSÉ

EAMON EVANS

THE STORIES BEHIND AUSTRALIA'S WEIRD AND WONDERFUL PLACE NAMES

hachette
AUSTRALIA

Aboriginal and Torres Strait Islander people are advised that this publication contains names and images of people who have passed away.

While all efforts have been made to acknowledge and contact owners of copyright for permission to reproduce their material, any copyright holders whose names have been unintentionally omitted from this book should contact the publisher to rectify the omission in subsequent editions.

Published in Australia and New Zealand in 2016
by Hachette Australia
(an imprint of Hachette Australia Pty Limited)
Level 17, 207 Kent Street, Sydney NSW 2000
www.hachette.com.au

10 9 8 7 6 5 4 3 2 1

Text copyright © Eamon Evans 2016
Illustrations copyright © Peter Broelman 2016

National Library of Australia
Cataloguing-in-Publication data:

Evans, Eamon, author.

Mount Buggery to Nowhere Else: the stories behind
Australia's weird and wonderful place names/Eamon Evans.

ISBN: 978 0 7336 3558 8 (paperback)

Names, Geographical – Australia – Miscellanea.
Curiosities and wonders.

919.40014

Cover design by bookdesignbysaso.com.au
Cover photograph courtesy of Lloyd Sutton/Alamy Stock Photo
Illustrations courtesy of Peter Broelman/broelman.com.au
Text design by Bookhouse, Sydney
Typeset in 11.5/17.4 pt Stempel Schneidler Std by Bookhouse, Sydney
Printed and bound in Australia by McPhersons Printing Group

CONTENTS

Introduction

'I've been everywhere, man.'

So sang '60s pop sensation Lucky Starr, in a song best enjoyed by the deaf.

But to my mind, Lucky was stretching it. Even if he really *had* been to all 94 of the Australian towns, regions, rivers and suburbs that his song sort of sometimes half-rhymes, that still leaves a fair number of places unaccounted for – and quite possibly Lucky-free.

Australia, as I imagine you've noticed, is really rather big. To truly go 'everywhere', you'd actually need to go to about four million places (including, alas, Perth and Geelong). You'd need to visit valleys and mountains, and drive through deserts and plains. You'd need to clamber over rocks, cross muddy creeks, and steer a boat between islands and bays. You'd need to buy maps and a compass, invest in boots and a backpack, and say goodbye to about half of your life.

I rather doubt that Lucky has done this – and, naturally, neither have I. Life is short, petrol is expensive, and there's just so much good stuff on TV.

But what I *have* done, dear reader, is spend time on Google, and run my eyes over a few books and maps. And in so doing, I have discovered something quite interesting. However boring many places in Australia might be, the names that we give them frequently aren't.

Take 'Snowtown', for example. Snowtown is a town with no snow.

Or 'Bordertown'. This one is far from the border.

Australia doesn't have any moles, and yet we have a 'Mole River', and while we have no monkeys, there's a 'Monkey Creek'. We don't grow oranges in 'Orange' or bananas in 'Banana', and there's no gate to keep you out of 'Bogan Gate'.

Interested yet? Well, what if I were to tell you that 'Dead Secret' really *does* have a secret, and that there was a real mystery at 'Mystery Bay'? Or that a ghost (or something like it) was once seen at 'Ghost Hill', just as 'Monster Creek' had a monster, of sorts.

But what can be found in 'Blood Creek'? Or, indeed, 'Coffin Bay' and 'Dead Mans Pass'? You'll need to read on if you want to know the answers – but take care in 'Murdering Gully' and 'Misery Bluff'.

On a cheerier note, we also have a town called Tittybong – though it's a bit of a disappointment (much like 'Mount Disappointment'), as there's nothing there but houses and shops. 'Rooty Hill' and 'Fiddletown' are perfectly respectable places as well, sad to say, just like 'Cockburn' and 'Upper Swan'.

From 'Horny Point' and 'Shag Island' to 'Mount Mee' and 'Iron Knob', Australia is full of places that *sound* very interesting and, well, kind of aren't.

But against that we have place names that *don't* sound interesting, but in fact have a story to tell. Behind the staid name of 'Fremantle' is the story of an aristrocratic rapist, while 'Sydney' dates back to the undead. Lord 'Melbourne' liked to whip orphan girls and Dr 'Bass' may not have been straight.

Want more? Well, sure. In *Mt Buggery to Nowhere Else*, you will discover that the king of 'Kings Cross' had his own royal sex chair, and Edward (Lake) 'Eyre' murdered dozens of kids. The 'Simpson Desert' is named after a man who made washing machines, and St Kilda was far from being a saint.

I could go on and on, and in actual fact I have. The result is the rest of this book. Australia's four million place names are filled with stories of hope and courage, and failure and cowardice, and murder and abduction. This is a book about starvation and shipwrecks, convicts and corruption, mutinies and daring escapes. It's a book about bungling bureaucrats and near-blind explorers, and brave animals who weren't all that bright. This is a book with fat kangaroos, peculiar smells, wombat poo and wallaby's urine.

It is, in other words, a book about Australia. I very much hope you enjoy it.

Australia

'What's in a name?' a girl called Juliet once asked her good chum Romeo.

When it comes to the land down under, the answer is 'Rather a lot'. Here's a little snapshot of how Australia came to be so called.

TERRA NULLIUS (60 000+ BC)

As big as Australia is today, there was a time when it was bigger still. Low sea levels meant that our wide, brown land was even wider – connected in the south to what's now Tasmania, and in the north to what's now Papua New Guinea. And it was also quite a bit less brown, with huge inland lakes and lush river valleys.

And then at some point, it got humans as well. Probably about 50 000 years ago (though, really, it's anyone's guess), an uncertain number of people arrived in an uncertain way for some reason that is – yes – uncertain. We *do* know that they came here from south-east Asia, probably as part of a group that then moved north to China. And we also know that, at some point after they arrived, this continent became both drier and more isolated as sea levels started to rise. The first Australians were effectively cut off from the world, and so set about making one of their own.

TERRA ANONYMOUS (60 000BC – 400BC)

We also don't know what they called that world. What was their name for 'Australia', if in fact they had one at all?

Fast forward 47 500 years and Australia still didn't have a name that we know of – though the same could be said for England and France. This is because, much like those nations, we weren't really a nation at all. We were, rather, about *250* nations, with at least as many languages and dialects.

And while it was one thing to name *your* nation's land or another nation's land, trying to give a name to *all* the land would, for an Indigenous person, have been like trying to cram all the mystery and magic and meaning of existence into a single word. The land is not just something the first Australians lived *on*; it is something that they lived *with* and *through*. As the anthropologist Deborah Rose in *Nourishing Terrains* put it, it is:

a living entity with a yesterday, today and tomorrow, with a consciousness, and a will toward life. People talk about country in the same way they would talk about a person:

they speak to country, sing to country, visit country, worry about country, feel sorry for country, and long for country. People say that country knows, hears, smells, takes notice, takes care, is sorry or happy. Because of this richness, country is home, and peace. It is nourishment for body, mind, and spirit.

Country is also:

multi-dimensional. It consists of people, animals, plants, Dreamings; underground, earth, soils, minerals and waters, surface water, and air. There is sea country and land country; in some areas people talk about sky country. Country has origins and a future; it exists both in and through time.

Can you come up with one word for all that? I'm pretty sure 'Australia' doesn't really cut it.

TERRA AUSTRALIS INCOGNITA (400BC – 500AD)

But the word 'Australia' is what we've ended up with, and it's more or less because of the ancient Greeks. Around the same time we're talking about (that is, around 400BC), most people in the know tended to know the Earth was not flat but rather a big round ball. But what use is a ball that's too heavy on top? A proper sphere should be properly balanced.

It was therefore postulated by Plato and the like, that – given that there was so much land spread across the north of the planet, from Asia to Africa and Europe – there must, in fact, be an equally big continent to provide a counterweight of some sort in the south.

Some philosophers called this pseudo-land 'the Antipodes', and if you've ever wondered why, just think of *pod*iatrists. 'Anti' means opposite and *podes* means 'feet'. If Athens and its neighbours were at the head of the planet, the unknown southern land beneath them must be its feet.

Mostly, however, they called it just that: *terra australis incognita*, a phrase meaning 'unknown southern land'.

And even though Terra Australis would remain incognito for many more centuries to come, it started appearing on maps, thanks to men like Macrobius, a 'Neoplatonist' from the fifth century AD. Ancient cartographers 'abhorred a vacuum', as Michael Pearson, author of *Great Southern Land: The Maritime Exploration of Terra Australis*, puts it, and would seize any excuse to draw land and not sea. Their maps tend to 'combine reliable survey with fanciful coastlines based on particular cosmological views, on vague and misinterpreted travellers' tales, or on the simple desire to fill up the map area with something, anything'.

Terra Australis varied wildly in size and shape, though it generally stayed near what's now known as the Antarctic.

TERRA WHO-THE-HELL-KNOWS? (500 - 1606)

So when did Terra Australis stop being 'a fanciful coastline' and become a continental fact? When, in other words, did non-Australians become cognisant that there really was a great land to the south, and give it some kind of name?

The annoying thing is that we really don't know. As Claire Corbett puts it in her essay 'Putting Australia on the Map: "Mapping Our World" at the National Library of Australia', 'The outline of Australia slowly emerges from the "dark sea" like a photograph developed in an old-fashioned chemical bath.'

Taking things chronologically, some say that the Vikings travelled here in the 1200s, and called us *Solar Partistra* ('the sunburnt land'). Others say that *Locach*, the land that Marco Polo wrote about the century after that, was in fact Australia (rather than Thailand).

Moving on, there's some chance that the Chinese came by. They certainly traded with what's now Indonesia, and put something not unlike northern Australia on a couple of four-teenth and fifteenth-century maps. But if any of them ever gave it a name, they didn't bother to write it down.

It would be a surprise if southern Indonesian fishermen weren't at least aware of our coastline (though God knows what they called it). There's even some evidence to suggest that the Macassans 'began annual voyages to the north coast of Western Australia, Northern Territory and Queensland well before recorded visits by the Europeans' – presumably to fish or to trade.

But let's get factual. When did those recorded visits begin?

Answer number 1 is 1504. It was then that a French sailor called Jean Binot Paulmier de Gonneville supposedly struck a 'violent storm' near the Cape of Good Hope, got lost, and drifted east for six weeks. He (somehow) found his way back to France the next year and claimed to have accidentally come across the fabled 'Austral land'. His preferred name for what he called his 'discovery' was *Indies Meridionale* (the South Indies), but chances are we call it Madagascar.

Fifteen years later, a Spaniard, Ferdinand Magellan, sailed below South America to 'discover' a new ocean which he called 'the Pacific'. He then sailed across it, in an effort to find a western sea route to Indonesia's Spice Islands – and some say that, on the way, he found Australia.

All we know for sure is that a continent called *Brasiliae Australis* appeared on a 1533 map of the world, along with a note describing it as 'recently discovered but not yet fully explored'. Though, as the name suggests, the cartographer put us south of Brazil . . . whereas, in fact, we're about 16000 kilometres west. It could be that he was talking about Antarctica. But, since he also wrote about how the 'good, honest . . . inhabitants of this region' named their children after 'St Thomas the Apostle', it could also be that he was just making stuff up.

What else? Well, yet another bunch of maps – these ones from the 1560s – feature yet another bunch of strange-looking, crudely sketched lands a little south-east of what's now Indonesia. Usually called *La grande île de Java* ('the great island of Java') – though other names included *Psittacorum region* (the 'Land of parrots'), *Magellanica* ('the land of Magellan') and *La Australia del Espíritu Santo* ('the southern land of the Holy Spirit') – these lands were by and large Spanish and Portuguese 'discoveries', though what they'd actually 'discovered' is anyone's guess. Probably just a few Pacific islands.

HOLLANDIA NOVA (1606-1770)

As you may have gathered by now, fifteenth- and sixteenth-century sailors were by and large sailing blind. Lacking any reliable way to work out their longitude, they were essentially unable to ever truly know where they were, let alone draw a good map.

Technology began to improve in the 1600s, just in time for the rise of the Dutch. While Portugal and Spain had hitherto dominated the south seas (thanks to their 'discovery' of South America), things got trickier when the Netherlands became an independent nation in 1581 and decided to make a play for the spice trade. They set up a trading port in what's now Indonesia, and – in a rather more systematic manner than their forebears – started to sniff around in the south.

And so came the moment we've been waiting for: the first *definite* 'discovery' of Australia in about 50 000 years. In 1606, a Dutch East India Company captain called Willem Janszoon sailed from Indonesia to what we can now be sure was Cape York – though at the time he thought he was seeing New Guinea.

The reason we can be sure is because, in the decades after Janszoon, the Dutch definitively charted the coasts of D'Edel's Land, Endracht's Land, Van Diemen's Land and de Witt's Land. Or, as they are rather better known today, the Northern Territory, the Pilbara, Tasmania and the Great Australian Bight.

But were any of these lands the fabled Terra Australis? For most of the Dutch, the answer was no. Under their watch,

Australia's now-charted north-west became known as New Holland (or *Hollandia Nova*, to use the more formal Latin). The great southern land must be further south, they figured – and hopefully a bit more great. While the Dutch continued to map New Holland for over a century, they never actually bothered to claim it. They found the land dry, hot, inhospitable and, worst of all, devoid of spices.

NEW HOLLAND / NEW SOUTH WALES (1770–1817)

Enter the English. When a certain Captain James Cook was ordered 'to proceed to the southward in order to make discovery of . . . a Continent or Land of great extent', his attitude was sceptical, at best.

'I do not believe such a thing exists, unless in a high latitude,' he wrote of the legendary Terra Australis, as the *Endeavour* crossed the Pacific in 1770. After two centuries of European voyages across vast empty seas, the ancient Greek vision of a Europe-Africa-and-Asia-sized continent was starting to seem like a major stretch.

Cook was thus not surprised when he arrived at the south-eastern coast of New Holland without having encountered another continent in the South Pacific – though he was also not slow to give it another name. When Governor Phillip arrived with the First Fleet 18 years later, it was in the British colony of New South Wales that he landed (though the continent's unwanted north-west was still known as New Holland).

TERRA AUSTRALIS (AGAIN)

And, for most of his life, Matthew Flinders used those terms too. But when he confirmed that New South Wales and New Holland constituted a continent in 1803, by becoming the first person to sail around it, he used a popular book about his voyage to argue that – since it was a single geographic entity – the continent needed a single name.

It is necessary to geographical precision, that so soon as New Holland and New South Wales were known to form one land, there should be a general name applicable to the whole; and this essential point having been ascertained in the present voyage, with a degree of certainty sufficient to authorise the measure, I have, with the concurrence of opinions entitled to deference, ventured upon the re-adoption of the original Terra Australis; and of this term I shall hereafter make use, when speaking of New Holland and New South Wales, in a collective sense.

So we're back to 'Great Southern Land', then? Why do that?

Because the combined continent of New South Wales/New Holland was as 'great' as any 'southern land' was ever likely to get. 'There is no probability that any other detached body of land, of nearly equal extent, will ever be found in a more southern latitude,' Flinders wrote in 1814, which was six years before the discovery of Antarctica . . . an even more southern continent that's nearly twice our size.

But, to be fair, Flinders also felt that Terra Australis had 'antiquity to recommend it' and would be 'less objectionable' to the Dutch than an Anglo name like, say, New South Wales.

AUSTRALIA (HURRAH!)

However, the navigator felt that the word 'Australia' would work better still. 'Had I permitted myself any innovation upon the original term it would have been to convert it into Australia; as being more agreeable to the ear, and an assimilation to the names of the other great portions of the earth,' Flinders wrote in his introduction to his book *A Voyage to Terra Australis*.

Flinders wasn't the first to think of the name (see the capsule below). Like *Magellanica*, *Brasiliae Australis* and the *Land of Parrots*, it had popped up here and there (in reference to pretty much anywhere) over the centuries, as a refreshing riff on the rather staid 'Southern Land'.

But he was the man who made it popular. The book was a hit all over the colony, and the new name wasn't too far behind. The Governor of New South Wales, Lachlan Macquarie, received a copy in 1817 and started to use 'Australia' in his correspondence within weeks. He then recommended that the name be formally adopted, and in 1824 the British Admiralty agreed. It was officially sanctioned in 1830, with the publication of *The Australia Directory* in Britain, and in a range of Admiralty Hydrographical Office publications.

Australians all let us rejoice, because we finally have a name!

Early Uses of the Term 'Australia'

1538 – Appears on a map by Belgian cartographer Gerardus Mercator, though as part of a phrase (*climata australia* or 'southern wind') rather than as a stand-alone proper noun.

1545 – Appears on a (wholly fanciful) map of the Southern Hemisphere in *Astronomia: Teutsch Astronomei*, a (sort of) scientific work by Cyriaco Jacob zum Barth.

1625 – Appears as 'Australia del Espíritu Santo' in the English translation of a Dutch work by Sir Richard Hakluyt – but perhaps by accident, as a spelling mistake. Hakluyt had actually been writing (in Dutch) about 'Austrialia del Espíritu Santo', an island which we now know as Vanuatu. A Spanish sailor had 'discovered' it in 1606, and named it after Spain's ruling Habsburg family, which also ruled Austria.

1638 – Appears in the index of a Dutch manuscript, *A General Description of the Indies* (though, oddly, not in the text).

1693 – Appears in the English translation of a French novel, *The Adventures of Jacques Sadeur*, in reference to an entirely mythical 'Southern Land'.

1756 – The word 'Australasia' appears for the first time in *History of the Navigation of Terra Australis* by Charles de Brosses.

1771 – Appears in Alexander Dalrymple's *An Historical Collection of Voyages and Discoveries in the South Pacific Ocean*, though in reference to the entire South Pacific region, rather than just New Holland.

1793 – Appears in George Shaw and Sir James Smith's *Zoology and Botany of New Holland*. They write about 'the vast island, or rather continent, of Australia, Australasia or New Holland,' even though Flinders had yet to fully establish that New South Wales and New Holland made up a continent.

1804 – Frequently used by Matthew Flinders in his letters and daily conversation and then again in *A Voyage to Terra Australis*, his popular 1814 book.

4 April 1817 – Appears for the first time in a formal document: a despatch from Governor Lachlan Macquarie to Lord Henry Bathurst, Britain's Secretary for the Colonies. Macquarie recommended that it be formally adopted later that year – and in 1824 the Admiralty finally agreed.

New South Wales

'I now once more hoisted English Coulers [sic] and in the Name of His Majesty King George the Third, took possession of the whole Eastern Coast from the above Latitude 38°S down to this place by the name of New South Wales.'

Thus reads Captain Cook's diary entry for 22 August 1770 – a day which saw him grab a Union Jack, stick it into the ground, and give the eastern half of New Holland a brand new name.

Also a slightly odd name. I mean, really, what the hell was he thinking?

To this day, we simply don't know. Was this supposed to be a 'new' version of the south of Wales or a new version of Wales in the Southern Hemisphere? And why *Wales*, anyway? That country is small, wet, green and hilly. We are big, dry, brown and flat. Cook had no family connections to Wales, or Welsh friends or patrons. Indeed, he'd never even *been* there, from what we can tell.

The best explanation seems to involve Canada, of all places: Cook had spent much of his career there, prior to taking the *Endeavour* on its long journey south. He would have been well aware, therefore, that there was a place named New South Wales on the south coast of Hudson Bay. Chances are he was just feeling lazy, and thought, 'What the hell, let's recycle that.'

Imaginative place names, after all, were not exactly Cook's speciality. As his ship made its way up the New South Wales coast, he commemorated one or two crewmates (Cape Banks, Point Solander) and drew a bit from the landscape (Red Point, Black Head, Smoky Cape). But by and large he stuck with the time-honoured method of naming stuff after people who might help his career. Batemans Bay, Byron Bay, Port Jackson, Port Stephens, Cape Hawke – all honour some Admiralty big shot who had the power to hire and fire.

And it was much the same story after 1788, when the First Fleet turned New South Wales into a colony. The most influential bigwigs by far when it came to dispersing favours down under were Colonial Secretaries and undersecretaries. Sydney itself, together with its suburbs of Castlereagh and Liverpool, were all named after men who held one of these posts. As were towns like Camden and Goulburn and Huskisson. And Maitland and Bathurst and Wellington. And Aberdeen and Glenelg. Not to mention the Murray River.

Though British prime ministers were still important, of course, which is why New South Wales has places like Pitt Town, Chatham, Portland and Grafton, along with the Hawkesbury River.

But it would be wrong to suggest that the first governors of New South Wales only ever named places after people they wished to suck up to. We should, in all fairness, also point out that they named lots of other places after themselves.

While the first governor, Arthur Phillip, is mostly remembered in what's now Victoria (Phillip Island, Port Phillip Bay), his successors managed to commandeer a fairly ludicrous chunk of what's now New South Wales. Governors John Hunter and Ralph Darling were bad enough (Hunters Hill, Hunter River, Hunter Valley, Darling River, Darling Harbour, Darling Downs, Darlinghurst, Darling Ranges, Darling Point), but the worst culprit was Lachlan Macquarie. You might think that Lake Macquarie, Macquarie Island, the Macquarie River, Port Macquarie and Macquarie Pass are enough Macquarie place names to be getting on with, but you are not Lachlan Macquarie. That governor also gave us Macquarie Fields, Macquarie Place and Macquarie Street, not to mention Mount Macquarie and the Macquarie Harbour.

Thankfully, however, governors couldn't go and name *everything* (which is why Sydneysiders don't live in Macquarie City in the state of New South Macquarie). Ordinary colonists were able to have a shot too, provided they owned, or at least settled, the land.

So how did they go about it? Well, a lot of the time settlers simply described where they were – New South Wales has its fair share of 'Green Valleys,' 'Main Creeks' and 'Big Hills' – but many settlers clearly liked to pretend they were somewhere else. Around 50 New South Wales towns and suburbs are named after places in England (think: Paddington, Penrith,

Kensington, Canterbury) and the number of Scottish place names isn't much lower.

Occasionally there's a sort of rough logic to this. New South Wales's Newcastle, like England's, is a city built on coal mines, while Putney, Richmond and Windsor are laid out along Sydney's rivers as their namesakes are along the Thames. But more often than not, there's no logic at all. Most British names seem to derive from the fact that some settler used to live there, or simply thought that it sounded quite nice.

Fortunately, however, they also thought that a lot of Indigenous names sounded nice.

'We were at first inclined to stigmatise this language as harsh and barbarous in its sounds,' said Watkin Tench, a settler who arrived with the First Fleet. 'Their combinations of words, in the manner they utter them, frequently convey such an effect. But if not only their proper names of men and places, but many of their phrases and a majority of their words, be simply and unconnectedly considered, they will be found to abound with vowels and to produce sounds sometimes mellifluous and sometimes sonorous.'

It's estimated that about three-quarters of all New South Wales place names have their origins in the 70 or so languages that greeted the original white settlers. While the Eora were the first people to be almost wiped out – dispossessed from their ancestral lands around Sydney; dying in droves from diseases like measles and smallpox – their language lives on in place names such as Parramatta, Maroubra and Cammeray.

As explorers and surveyors ventured north, east and west to establish towns like Woy Woy and Wollongong, they were often instructed as a matter of policy to use Indigenous place names wherever they could. 'You will be particular in noting the native names of as many places as you can on your map of that part,' surveyor-general Sir Thomas Mitchell wrote in 1828. 'The great convenience of using native names is obvious . . . So long as any of the Aborigines can be found in the neighbourhood . . . future travellers may verify your map, whereas new names are of no use in this respect.'

But while it's great that so many Indigenous languages can at least be seen on our maps, we can't really be sure *what* we're seeing half the time – or even that they're Indigenous at all.

For one thing, the vast majority of the languages that greeted the settlers are no longer understood. Records may suggest that 'Woy Woy' means 'Place of much water' in Darkinjung, for example, but since there are no longer any people who can actually speak Darkinjung, who knows if that's actually true.

And the name might not even be 'Woy Woy'. 'In most cases, the Indigenous names were first recorded by people with little knowledge of the language concerned, and . . . altered to conform more closely with English phonology or typical name-shapes.' 'Woy Woy' might have been 'Boy Boy' or 'Foy Foy'. Or 'Waiyi Waiyi', or God knows what else.

And even if Woy Woy *was* indeed Woy Woy, it might have been 'Tuggeranong' and 'Toolibin' as well. Indigenous culture was far from homogenous. Any given place might have had a dozen different names, and have been inhabited by multiple nations.

Ready for one last layer of complication? Well, sorry, but you're going to get it anyway. As Flavia Hodges of the Australian National Placenames Survey (ANPS) points out, 'similar sounding words in one Indigenous language might mean something else in another. Even in the same language, similar names became confused.' The result is that 'as the Europeans attempted to record Indigenous place names, the spellings and meanings often became hopelessly muddled . . .' In other words, 'Woy Woy' might well be a Darkinjung phrase meaning 'Place of much water' – but the place itself might have been named by another nation, in whose language 'Woy Woy' meant something else.

Sorry. My head hurts too.

Based at Macquarie University, the ANPS is nonetheless hoping to un-muddle things. The national database that the organisation is working on promises to 'record all known Australian names, documenting their pronunciation, generic class, status (gazetted, obsolete, non-gazetted, sensitive, disputed etc.), origin, meaning, history, cultural significance (of both name and site), and map reference and location.'

Unfortunately, it also promises to be a bit boring. In these pages, I'm giving you the fun stuff.

ADAMINABY

Some stories behind place names are just so ridiculous that, to my mind, they might just be true.

Such is the case with Adaminaby, a small town near the Snowy Mountains which started out as a small gold mine. Said mine was apparently owned by a man who, like so many, was a touch scared of his wife. Not being able to placate her with chocolates, or find a shop that sold roses or rosé, he rather romantically gave her a legal document that meant the mine was now owned in her name.

'Ada's mine it be,' the peacemaker softly proclaimed.

BEARDY PLAINS

As a beard wearer of many years standing, I know it's not a fashion choice that comes without risks. Let it go too hairy and you look like a hobo – or a hipster, which could well be worse.

But on the upside, a beard may make you immortal (as well as disguising a weak chin). As evidence, I present Beardy Plains, an area in northern New South Wales which also features Beardy River and a Beardy Hill. They all got their name from two bearded stockmen, Bill Chandler and John Duval, who lived there in the 1830s and '40s, doing whatever it is that stockmen do.

Anyone who was thinking about moving north was advised to consult them, as only 'the beardies' knew the lay of the land.

BINNAWAY

Not all place names make a whole lot of sense. And then there are a few that make absolutely none.

Binnaway, for example, got its name from 'binna' and 'wai' . . . two local Indigenous terms meaning 'ear' and 'to throw away'. So who threw an ear away? Whose ear was it? And why? Your guess is as good as mine.

BIRAGANBIL

We Australians rightly treasure our fauna: the koalas and kangaroos, wombats and wallabies, kookaburras sitting in the old gum trees, and all sorts of other unique and precious species that have at this present moment slipped my mind.

But not all of them belong in a brochure. Most tourists who come to this wide brown land would probably be content to leave it without visiting Biraganbil (a 'place of leeches') or Burrimul (a 'place of blowflies').

Tooloom, for its part, offers tourists 'lice and ticks', while Bugilbone is 'the place of the death adder'.

And if you have some spare time, don't use it to visit Coolatai, 'the place of rock adders', or indeed Tooraweenah, where there are 'plenty of brown snakes'.

BLACKTOWN

Did you know that the United States has a 'Negro Mountain'? Not to mention a 'Darkey Springs' and a 'Dago Peak'? Or that in France there's a hamlet called 'La Mort aux Juifs' (charming translation: 'the death of the Jews')?

But fear not, folks, Australia's still pulling its weight: casual racism is one of the many things this country does well. Take the Sydney suburb of Blacktown, for example. Supposedly named after a 'Native Institute' where Aboriginal children were once schooled, it's been raising eyebrows for about 100 years now, and will probably raise them for 100 more . . .

BLAND SHIRE

A rose by any other name might smell as sweet, but if it was called a 'snot-vomit,' no-one would buy it. Good branding is everything, as marketing types like to tell us, but a quick study of some of New South Wales's towns, shires and regions shows that some of us simply aren't listening.

Quite apart from Bland Shire – an area named after a Dr William Bland – the state has Coonamble, which means 'a place of bullock dung' and Goonambil, whose name simply means 'excrement'. Inglegar was named after some 'sick people', and Wahgonga for its stinging nettles.

I could go on and on. In fact, I think I will. Real estate agents also have a tough time in Gooallie ('ugly') and Taloumbi ('windy'), and I suspect that many of them would struggle in Kouming, which comes from a phrase meaning 'scum on the eye'.

BLUE MOUNTAINS

'The more I know, the more I realise how little I know,' said someone (I don't know who).

And when it comes to the Blue Mountains, he or she was right. All of us know that said mountains get their name from the blueish tinge they take on from a distance, thanks to the eucalyptus oil that evaporates from the gum trees and somehow colours the light. (For a full explanation of this complex scientific phenomenon, you'll need to get your head around concepts like 'Mie scattering' and 'volatile terpenoids' and then buy a different book.)

Anyway, we may all be right about this. But we might also be quite wrong.

Another perfectly credible theory about the name 'Blue Mountains' is that it's simply borrowed from a place overseas. Many of the British naval officers who came to Australia in the early days came here straight from Jamaica. That then-British colony also has a 'Blue Mountains' which looked (and still looks) rather similar.

BOBLEDIGBIE

'A kick on the bottom.'

BOGAN GATE

There's nothing wrong with a town full of bogans, if it's surrounded by a high, locked gate. Despite this promising name, however, the residents of Bogan Gate can, in fact, come and go as they please.

But don't worry, they're not (all) bogans. The name actually comes from a local Aboriginal word meaning 'the birthplace of a notable headman of the local tribe'.

Or that's what they tell us, anyway . . .

BOONOO BOONOO

'Bad country.'

BOTANY BAY

Farewell to old England forever,
farewell to my rum culls as well.
Farewell to the well-known Old Bailey,
where I once used to cut such a swell.
Singing too-ral-li, oo-ral-li, addity.
Singing too-ral-li, oo-ral-li, ay.
Singing too-ral-li, oo-ral-li, addity,
and we're bound for Botany Bay.

Setting aside the question of why anyone would sing 'too-ral-li, oo-ral-li, addity' – what on earth do those words even *mean*? – it's worth noting that the convicts who came here from England were not bound for Botany Bay at all.

That was the original idea, of course, Sir Joseph Banks having recommended the place as eminently suitable for a penal settlement and series of farms. The bay's 'lush pastures' and 'well-watered and fertile grounds' were so very lush, well-watered and fertile, in fact, that Cook even named it after botany, the science of plants.

But when the First Fleet arrived, just 18 years later, the Botany Bay colony lasted less than a week. It quickly became clear that the area was unsuitable for crops, so everybody hopped back in the boats and sailed to Sydney Cove.

BREAKFAST POINT

Breakfast is not usually a social time (try to talk during mine and I may well shoot you), but there are exceptions to every rule.

One such exception occurred in 1788 when one Captain John Hunter (from whom Hunters Hill gets its name) became the first white man to see members of the Wangal clan at a place he called Breakfast Point.

'We landed to cook breakfast on the opposite shore to them,' Hunter later wrote, 'made signs to them to come over and waved green boughs. Soon after which, seven of them came over in two canoes and landed near our boats. They left their spears in the canoes and came to us. We tied beads etc. about them and left them [the remains of] our fire.'

COAL AND CANDLE CREEK

Want to hear an interesting story involving some coal and a candle? Well, you're not going to get it here. This little Sydney creek was named after a famous British soldier called Colin Campbell (say it out loud . . .), who is clearly not so famous today.

But if you're prepared to travel about 100 kilometres south, and abandon any interest in candles, I can at least tell you a story about coal. In 1797, you see, a cargo ship called the *Sydney Cove* crashed into some rocks a little north of Tasmania. Bloodied but unbowed, the crew set off in the ship's little long-boat in the direction of Sydney Cove itself.

On the way, however, they managed to sink their boat yet again, near what's now called Ninety Mile Beach. Sydney was still 600 kilometres away, so (by now fairly bowed) they rolled their eyes and started to walk.

It was, as you might imagine, a long way to trek, and it's thought that a dozen of them died. But on the upside, they discovered coal exposed in a cliff, and were thus able to light a fire, attracting rescuers. The area is now called Coalcliff, and this anecdote is now at an end.

COME BY CHANCE

Life is full of surprises, so long as you're easily surprised.

It seems that George and William Colless were two such people. So stunned were these two sheep farmers when they got the opportunity to purchase a small piece of land, they decided to name said land 'Come By Chance', to commemorate Fortuna, fickle goddess of luck.

CONCORD

Concord, the word, means harmony – a coming together of different views into a warm, soft and cosy group hug.

Whoever gave the name to the Sydney suburb was most likely copying Concord, the US town. That town is very well-known, after all, as having been the place where the War of Independence began ...

COOGEE

Lots of tourists come to Coogee beach, but so too does decaying kelp. The tide washes it in every day, and things can get pretty pungent if it doesn't wash back out.

Or that's what the Aborigines thought, anyway. Coogee means 'smelly place'.

COONONG

'Dirty water.'

COUTTS CROSSING

Anyone who's shopped at a supermarket knows what it is to eat terrible bread. But even *their* bland white blobs of tastelessness may well be preferable to a loaf baked in the 1840s, if the flour came from one Thomas Coutts.

This Coutts, you see, was a sheep farmer – and no fan of Indigenous folks. His ongoing feud with a local tribe, whose hunting ground he had turned into paddocks, culminated in him putting arsenic into a sackful of flour and leaving it out on his porch.

Sure enough, it was soon gone, and somewhere between seven and 20 people then died.

And if you're wondering how many years Coutts then spent in gaol, the answer is somewhere between zero and none.

CRACKENBACK RANGE

Without wanting to generalise in any way, shape or form, I think it's safe to say that hikers are weird. I mean, what on earth is fun about clambering up a snake-strewn, fly-infested series of cliffs, while hauling a backpack under a blazing sun? Is it the promise of flatbread and cup-a-soup, or is it the cold night in a tent that appeals?

Anyway, whatever their 'reasons' might be, I'm sure that even the most masochistic of hikers might feel a twinge of regret halfway up Crackenback Range. Those mountains above Thredbo are so very steep, they could easily crack a person's back.

CROPPY POINT

Back in the 1960s, polite society shunned 'longhairs'. There was nothing worse than those sandal-wearing, peace-loving hippy types, with their soppy love songs and long, flowing locks.

But in the early 1800s, things were reversed: it was the *short-hairs* who were the source of all problems. For this was a time when the people who were powerful and wealthy wore wigs, just as French aristocrats had done pre-guillotine. Cropping your hair short was a way to express support for the Revolution, or at least cock a snook at the snobby.

It's said that three such 'croppys' – Irish convicts on the run – once set up camp on the banks of the Hawkesbury, at what is now called Croppy Point.

CUMBERLAND STATE FOREST

Having a good personality is clearly important, but good blood lines can matter more. Rewarded for his by having Cumberland State Forest named after him, the Duke of Cumberland was not a good person, but since his father was the King of England it would seem that no-one much cared.

An arch-Tory with an autocratic manner, scarred face and scandalous past, the 'Hanoverian Ogre' was accused of raping his sister, rorting an election, and murdering his valet in a fit of rage. (All we know for sure about the last charge was that the servant was found in bed with a slashed throat, and only his master had actually been in the house.)

Cumberland is also said to have driven a man to suicide through having an affair with the man's wife, and to have once instructed his driver to run over two small girls, on the grounds that they were blocking his carriage.

DANCING DICKS CREEK

Who was Dick and why did he dance? I'm sorry, but I simply don't know.

All I *can* tell you is that he was not alone. Dick lived in a state that also has a Happy Dicks Creek (in Jingera) and a Hopping Dicks Creek (in Tweed).

Guyra, for its part, has a Stuttering Dicks Creek, while Bowna has no such problems. That Riverina community is pronounced 'boner'.

DARLINGHURST

The seventh governor of New South Wales, Sir Ralph Darling, was once described by the *Sydney Morning Herald* as 'a tyrant outranked only by the Great Moghul, the Tsar and the Emperor of China'.

And some would say that they were being kind. 'The most unpopular personage in the colony', the 'spiteful' and 'obstinate' Darling is said to have 'ruled the convicts with a rod of iron' and 'stretched the authority he possessed to the verge of abuse'.

Still, nobody is all bad (well, almost nobody) and we should note that Darling at least knew how to be self-effacing. Sure, he may have named Darling Harbour, Darling Point, Darling Street, Darling River and the Darling Downs after himself, but the suburb of 'Darlinghurst', despite what you might think, had nothing to do with him at all.

No, sir – he named it after his wife . . .

DEAD SECRET

Being dead doesn't have too many benefits (apart from meaning that you'll never see another reality TV show).

And another benefit, now I think of it, is that it makes it much easier to keep a secret. According to a 1947 article in the *Sydney Morning Herald*, there's 'a locality just outside Dubbo' that locals have given a rather strange name. As the report has it:

> Many years ago, a prospector walked into Dubbo and showed a number of people some of the finest gold specimens ever seen in the town. He refused to divulge the spot where he found the gold but after getting a stock of provisions, set out to work his new claim. A few days later he was found dead in a patch of scrub, the gold specimens beside his body. Thus he took the secret of his find to the grave. Many searched without success to locate the gold, and since then the place has always been known as The Dead Secret.

DEE WHY

Who built the Easter Island statues, and was there a second gunman on the grassy knoll? Is there a God, or life on another planet, and will we ever see an end to reality TV? These are just some of the great and enduring mysteries that continue to occupy our planet's great minds.

Other minds, such as my own, are focused on smaller matters. For example, why would someone name a suburb

Dee Why? The name apparently comes from the notebook of one James Meehan, a surveyor charged with carving up Sydney's northern beaches. In the relevant page, Meehan jotted down two words, 'Dy Beach', and to this day, no-one knows why.

Theories? Well, it could be a local Aboriginal word (which doesn't seem likely) or an abbreviation for 'dirty' (less likely still). Another idea is that it was half a reference to 'dy/dx', a derivative in calculus (which sounds impressive but makes next to no sense).

All we know for a fact is that 'Dy' is now pronounced 'Dee' and 'Why' – probably because the alternative was a little too morbid.

DENILIQUIN

A little town close to the Murray, with all sorts of lovely lagoons, Deniliquin got its name 'from a local Aboriginal chief known as Denilakoon who was noted for his size, strength and wrestling'.

DEVILS BACKBONE

Whether or not the Devil lurks within all of us, he's certainly lurking in New South Wales. Not only does the horned one have it in for the state's hikers (try climbing up Devils Backbone and you may not climb down), he is also hard at work underground. 'Devils Hole campground and picnic area offers picnicking, wildlife, scenic views, and fishing,' says the NSW Tourist Board, but they fail to add that it's a straight drop to Hell.

New South Wales also boasts alternative routes to fiery torment, such as 'Devils Bend' and 'Hells Hollow Swamp'.

And while no-one quite knows why 'Satans Toe Swamp' is so named, I can tell you that 'Wandoo Wandong' and 'Boonbollong' are both best avoided, as both mean 'The Evil One'.

DOGANABUGANARAM

Dogs may well be man's best friend, but we don't mind having more.

Visitors to New South Wales have a long list of animal-inspired place names to check out (should they ever choose to leave Sydney and Byron). Take Whale Beach and Wombat Creek, for example, along with Deer Vale and Kangaroo Flat.

You could consider visiting Cow Flat or plump for Duck Creek – or perhaps Green Pigeon or Pelican Point.

But the true animal lover has only one choice: to head straight to Doganabuganaram. It's said that a surveyor once camped there, all alone but for a dog and a bug and a ram.

EBENEZER

Shall we just take it as read that you've studied the Bible, and know the Book of Samuel like the back of your hand? Well, can I direct your attention to the bit where 'Samuel took a stone and set it between Mizpah and Shen, and named it Ebenezer'?

Now, I myself have not studied the Bible and so have no idea who Samuel was or why he would do this. But the result of his rock placement, I am told, is that the name 'Ebenezer' now means 'stone of help'.

The residents of one of New South Wales's oldest and prettiest towns adopted the name around 1815, being proud of their old and pretty stone church.

EULOMOGO

'Without fingernails.'

FARM COVE

It would be wrong to say that very little planning went into the settlement of Sydney Cove. Everything was planned within an inch of its life – it just wasn't planned very well.

Governor Phillip's 'ineffectual incompetence' was perhaps at its most mind-boggling at a place called Farm Cove. Now home to Sydney's Botanic Garden, the cove's sandy soil was home to Australia's very first farm . . . and also its first farm to fold. With only one farmer aboard the First Fleet, and no crops that were even half-suitable, the colonists came close to starving in 1788, and closer still in the two years that followed.

It was only when someone thought to colonise Parramatta that some crops finally began to grow, and the First Fleet could stop eating rats, crows and dogs.

FARMERS CREEK

According to namenerds.com, a vaguely plausible-looking website, 'Jessie' and 'Sam' are Australia's preferred dog names, and we like to call our cats 'Tiger' and 'Puss'.

It's fortunate that 'Farmer' isn't high on the list, for (without wanting to sound in any way superstitious) I must tell you that that name is doomed.

The proof lies near Lithgow (or at least did, until it decomposed). It's said that a nineteenth-century surveyor once had a horse called 'Farmer', which somehow managed to drown in the Murrumbidgee River. Forced to buy another horse, the surveyor gave it the exact same name, and vowed to take better care of it.

But this horse somehow managed to drown too, falling into a little creek and breaking its neck. The surveyor named said waterway 'Farmers Creek'. And then named his next horse something else.

FIDDLETOWN

Minds out of the gutter, readers: this is not what you think at all.

A semi-rural suburb of Sydney, Fiddletown was settled by three sprightly young bachelors who were all rather fond of a fiddle. Every single night, it is said, they liked to get together and bang out some lively tunes. When more settlers arrived, they would play their fiddles for them too, and at some stage the name was born.

Mind you, Fiddletown isn't the only place in New South Wales that might attract the wrong type of guest. The state also boasts a Licking Hole Creek and a Bumbaldry mine, a Dicks Hill and a Bobbin Head.

The town of Buttaba, meanwhile, can be found a bit north of Booti Booti, and not all that far east of Bong Bong.

FIELD OF MARS

'Mars' was the Roman god of war. Fond of strutting about stark naked but for a big beard and spear, this bloodthirsty deity is why we have 'martial arts', not to mention 'Mars', the blood-red planet.

He's presumably also why we have the 'Field of Mars Reserve' in north-western Sydney, though nobody is quite sure about the connection.

The name is thought to have come from Governor Phillip (as dubious ideas so often did). The most likely explanation is that he had granted some land there to a couple of former marines.

FISHERS GHOST CREEK

When somebody says they've seen a ghost, the correct response is to smile politely and then slowly back away.

But when a 'respectable local man' said just this to a policeman in 1826, said policeman did more than just smile. He actually agreed to go and take a look at the paddock where the ghost had supposedly been seen.

Perhaps this was because the ghost had apparently looked like Fred Fisher – another respectable local man, who had recently left town. According to his good friend George Worrall, to whom Fisher had given much of his land, he had gone to the Mother Country to try his luck there.

But Worrall, as it turned out, was not such a good friend, for the policeman found Fisher's body very near where his 'ghost' had been, decomposing in what's now Fishers Ghost Creek.

It didn't take the police too long to arrest Worrell – or too much torture to make him confess. He was hanged by the neck in 1827. And Fisher's ghost is still seen to this day.

FOLLY POINT

I don't know much about building things, but I certainly know not to try it myself. This is apparently more than one particular Sydneysider ever knew.

It's said that this man kept on trying to build a house on what's now called Folly Point, only to see it collapse every single time. The problem, apparently, was that he kept using salt water in the mortar. Remember, kids: don't do it yourself.

GINS LEAP

If we disregard certain politicians, and our (less than) warm welcome of refugees, it seems fair to say that racism in Australia is . . . at least becoming a bit less explicit. The 'N' word, for example, is very much out of vogue: 'Little Nigger Creek' was recently renamed 'Little Gin Creek' by some enlightened residents of Far North Queensland.

But 'all things in moderation' must have been their approach in this matter, because it just so happens that 'gin' is a racist word too. Possibly derived from 'Aboriginal', it was a term white settlers once applied to Indigenous women – not least, the ones they intended to rape.

'Stockmen used to go out for a "gin spree",' according to Xavier Herbert. 'They'd run the blacks down and take the young girls [who'd] sit down and fill their fannies with sand.'

All of which helps explain why there's a cliff in New South Wales that goes by the name of 'Gins Leap'. It marks the spot where an Indigenous girl despairingly leapt to her death.

GOODNIGHT

According to AW Reed, 'this peculiar name was derived from an incident when the captain of a river steamer on the Murray heard a voice calling from the bank, "Goodnight!" Ever afterwards, he called that particular spot "the place where the bloke said 'Goodnight'".'

GORE HILL

The ABC, as the Murdoch press knows, is nothing less than a lefty plot.

If some media types had their way, the ABC's TV studios would never have been built at Gore Hill, and everyone who ever worked there would now be in gaol.

All of which perhaps makes it ironic that Gore Hill was named after a political prisoner. Considered an ally of the deposed governor, William Bligh, William Gore was arrested during the 'Rum Rebellion' and sent to prison for no real reason at all. He was released years later, after a new governor arrived and declared his trial completely invalid.

GOVERNORS KNOB

The dictionary defines a knob as 'a rounded hill, mountain or elevation on a ridge', and that's clearly not funny at all. So there's absolutely no reason to smirk at Governors Knob near Nombi, or indeed Chinamans Knob, south of Booral.

El Capitan Knob in Tinderay is another place to avoid jokes in, just as one naturally would if one visited Nimbin's Blue Knob.

GRONG GRONG

'Bad land.'

GUNDAGAI

Whatever you might see on the road to Gundagai, the road *from* it was once splattered with blood. The New South Wales town's name comes from 'gundabandoo-bingee,' a phrase meaning 'cut with a hand-axe at the back of the knee'.

HAT HEAD

A nice little town near a green, hilly headland, 'Hat Head' has a uniquely bad name, although 'Bonnet Bay' comes pretty close. Both places were thought to resemble headwear, though I suspect that whoever thought this was wearing dark sunglasses, had their eyes closed and was thinking of hats.

HATTONS BLUFF

According to at least one book, which I'm not entirely sure I believe, this nature reserve in north-eastern New South Wales was used as a sort of holiday retreat from time to time by a Mr Bill Hatton. 'The legend says the local Aboriginal people would burn his hut down while he was away and he bluffed that he would build a concrete and stone palace.'

Sounds very relaxing . . .

JERILDERIE

Some anecdotes deserve to live on in history, so inspired is their use of wordplay, so delicate, yet powerful, their wit.

The anecdote behind 'Jerilderie' does not fall into this category, but what the hell, let's tell it anyway. According to language experts, the town where Ned Kelly wrote his famous letter was probably named after 'Djirrildhuray', an Indigenous word meaning 'reedy place'.

But according to locals, it's because one of its first settlers was a man called Gerald, and his wife called him 'Gerald, dearie'.

KEARNS

Alexander the Great and Alexandria. Peter the Great and Saint Petersburg. From the Washington of George Washington to the Jaipur of Jai Singh, history has seen lots of Great Men go and found a great city and, with great gall, name it after themselves.

Kearns, on the other hand, is not a great city. And it would be hard to argue that Bill Kearns was a particularly great man. The first white settler in this small Sydney suburb, he became famous during an 1824 court case, in which it was alleged that he had impregnated a 14-year-old girl.

Fortunately, the girl's father, a Mr Joseph Ward, then returned from overseas. But it just so happened that he was an awful man too. Having got married himself while in the United Kingdom, Mr Ward now had no room for his actual wife and promptly told her to leave. His pregnant daughter, however, he decided to sell. And he got a good price from an American sea captain.

KING GEORGE SOUND

Do you remember a movie called *The Madness of King George*? Well, that was *this* King George.

Probably due to a genetic blood disorder called porphyria (though, really, it's anyone's guess) the monarch who lost the American colonies lost his mind more than once during his

60-year reign. In between years of being completely sane (and, if anything, slightly dull), George III endured long bouts of mistaking inanimate objects for friends, and talking at great speed in 500-word sentences.

'There were times when he would talk so much and so quickly that he would begin to foam at the mouth, needing to be restrained . . . And there were times when he thought that he was already dead, and he would have conversations with relatives who had long since passed on, and with the angels that surrounded him in heaven.'

KINGS CROSS

Sydney's seediest nightspot gets its name from our seediest king.

Originally named 'Queens Cross', to celebrate Queen Victoria's fiftieth year on the throne, this intersection of William Street, Darlinghurst Road and Victoria Street had a bit of a problem in the nineteenth century, insofar as it kept getting confused with Queens Square.

So when Edward VII came to the throne in 1901, a name change duly came to Queens Cross. And in the century that followed, lots of prostitutes came along too.

But don't worry, Edward would have approved. While he was certainly fond of drinking and gambling and eating too much, that sovereign's favourite pastime was definitely sex. He's thought to have slept with thousands of women, including in such places as a silk-lined coffin and a swan-shaped bath, which he liked to fill with champagne.

But the massively overweight Edward did his best work on a specially designed 'royal sex chair', a contraption with holes and straps and strategically placed slopes which let him have sex with two or more prostitutes without squashing a single one.

'I've spent enough on you to build a battleship,' he once complained to one of his mistresses, Lillie Langtry.

'Yes,' the actress is said to have replied, 'and you've spent enough *in* me to float one!'

LEICHHARDT

On 3 April 1848, the 'prince of explorers' set out from McPherson's station in southern Queensland in the company of six men, seven horses, 20 mules and 50 bullocks.

They were never seen again. What happened to Ludwig Leichhardt and his party remains a mystery to this day. The closest thing we have to a clue is a small brass plate with his name on it, found about 2000 kilometres to the station's west.

LINGER AND DIE HILL

I'm no real estate expert, but I suspect that land values could probably be higher around Linger and Die Hill if somebody changed its name.

Found at the end of 'a gravel road somewhere near Dungog' (a small town that's near nothing at all), the hill got its name from the timber workers who used to chop wood somewhere nearby. Hauling their logs away meant hauling them up and down the hill, which they would do with a big team of bullocks. But – since the hill was so steep, and the log-laden wagons so heavy – it was said that if just one bullock was to slow down for one moment, a terrible accident would quickly ensue.

LOOK AT ME NOW HEADLAND

Self-obsessed people don't really stick out like they used to, because the rest of us are all too self-obsessed to notice them.

But back in the nineteenth century, before Facebook and Twitter and reality TV, a bit of narcissism could really get a person noticed. And thus it was with an anonymous Englishman who was seeking to impress some colonial girls with his riding skills. 'Look at me now!' he reportedly said from his saddle, on a headland just north of Coffs Harbour. He then fell off the saddle, straight into the mud, and look at him they all did.

MACDONALDTOWN

Fortunately for local health workers, not to mention Australian culture in general, the Sydney suburb Macdonaldtown is not named after restaurants that sell Chicken McNuggets.

The name instead comes from something even more socially unacceptable: a former convict who dabbled in forgery. This Macdonald inherited the land from a Nicholas Erskine.

Or at least, that's what Erskine's 'will' said.

MACKSVILLE

'Good relationships involve compromise' is something I like to say to my partner when it becomes clear I'm losing an argument. It's better to have something at least a bit one's own way than to fight on and lose all.

A shining example of such relationship management can be seen in the town of Macksville. It wasn't named after just one of its first settlers, it was named after them *both*.

Angus Mackay and Hugh McNally 'were asked by the surveyor to give it a name, so they decided to call it Macksville, short for Macks' village'.

MACQUARIE

For true immortality, don't worry about the history books – just try to get your name on a road map instead.

If you don't believe me, just ask Lachlan Macquarie, a governor of New South Wales back in the days when it really was new. During 11 short years in office, he gave us a Macquarie Island and three Macquarie rivers, a Port Macquarie and a Lachlan River. That tireless worker also lent his name to three Macquarie streets and two suburbs called Macquarie, a Macquarie Park and a Macquarie Pass. You'll find his name on a lighthouse and a harbour and a university. And a hospital and on all sorts of hills.

The inscription on his tomb describes him as 'the father of Australia', though it's worth noting that that tomb is in Scotland. The good governor left Australia the first second he could, sailing out from Macquarie Wharf.

MANLY

Manliness is an elusive quality in the modern world. Must a real man drink beer and use power tools, or am I allowed to sip white wine while I watch *Will and Grace*?

In 1788, however, it was more straightforward: all you had to do to advertise your testosterone was learn how to throw a big spear. When a Guringai man did just this – grazing Arthur Phillip's epaulet-strewn shoulder – the governor was so impressed by his 'confidence and manly bearing' that he named the area Manly Cove.

MARSDEN PARK

One of Marsden Park's first white residents was a magistrate who often saw red. Known to history as 'the hanging parson', and to his contemporaries as a bit of a prick, the Reverend Samuel Marsden was a magistrate who liked to punish sinners, and then punish them quite a bit more.

Irish-Catholic convicts were his particular bugbear. He considered them 'a most wild, ignorant and savage race'. With 'minds Destitute of every Principle of Religion & Morality . . . they are very dangerous members of Society', Marsden once advised his superiors, in the course of suggesting that the religion be banned.

MINCHINBURY

When it came to appointing administrators in the early days of New South Wales, some people might say that talent was a little thin on the ground. But, my friends, they would be wrong: talent was pretty much non-existent.

This is why a ten-carat chump like William Minchin ended his career at the head of the Bank of New South Wales and as chief of the state's police.

The man after whom the suburb of Minchinbury is named started his career as a sea captain, taking charge of a ship full of female convicts. Despite them all being below decks, and, well, prisoners in chains, it was the only convict ship in history to successfully stage a mutiny. Minchin and a handful of sailors and soldiers were all set adrift on a raft.

After answering charges of incompetence in London, Minchin's next stop was New South Wales, where he wrongly accused a fellow administrator of corruption, and helped facilitate an illegal duel. But his greatest achievement was being the man in charge of Government House the day that dozens of rioters easily broke in and found Governor Bligh hiding under the bed.

MOLE RIVER

You can find a lot of information about Mole River online, including the fact that it has an elevation of over 600 metres. The web will also tell you that this 'watercourse of the Dumaresq-Macintyre catchment within the Murray Darling basin' runs for 73 kilometres through the Northern Tablelands, and has something called a 'source confluence' at Bluff River.

But what the web *won't* tell you, no matter how hard you look, is why the hell it was named after a mole. After all, outside of zoos and museums, moles are not often seen on our shores.

Platypuses, however, do live in Australia, and it turns out that people used to call them 'water moles' – though this was only after they were prepared to concede that platypuses actually exist. 'The platypus was first scientifically described by Dr George Shaw in Britain in 1799,' according to the good folk at the Australian Platypus Conservancy.

His initial reaction to the first specimen was that it was an elaborate hoax. It was not uncommon at the time for exotic forgeries (such as mermaids made by joining the body of a monkey to that of a fish) to be brought back to Europe from far-flung parts of the world. Shaw was so convinced that the platypus specimen had been fabricated that he took a pair of scissors to the pelt, expecting to find stitches attaching the bill to the skin.

MONARO

A long, expensive and high-level research project at the University of Wellington recently came up with a startling conclusion: men like looking at boobs.

They could have saved a whole lot of time and just bought an atlas. According to the toponymy expert AW Reed, New South Wales has at least five different places which at some point reminded some guy of norks. They include the district of Monaro ('"breasts of a woman", so named from the cone-shaped pinnacles in the vicinity') and of course the Namoi River ('from nynamu, the breast, because the river here curves like a woman's breast').

And next time you visit Nea, Kooroomie or Mudah, please remember: their eyes are up here.

MONKEY CREEK

Monkeys, as we all know, come from Africa and Asia. But could some now-extinct species of them have once roamed our wide brown land?

It's an intriguing question to which the answer is, 'Sorry, no.' It turns out that *koalas* were often called 'monkey bears' until someone came up with a better name.

MOOBALL

'A visit to northern New South Wales is not complete without visiting the cute town of Mooball,' says a journalist with questionable taste. Mooball's attractions include electricity poles painted with black and white cow prints and a general store with 'some interesting "Mooey" things to purchase'. And, well, that's about it, really, unless we include a road sign that 'makes one have a chuckle' as it reads 'Hoo Roo from the Moo Moo'.

It all, to my mind, lends some weight to the argument that 'Mooball' is an Indigenous word meaning 'bowels'.

MOPPIN

A local word for 'thigh'. And no-one knows why.

MOSMAN

Australia may have 'ridden on the sheep's back' to wealth, as someone once delicately put it, but we started out on top of a whale. Whales were big business, back in the days when various of their body products were used to light lamps and make candles and soap and perfume.

Sydney Cove became a harpooning hot spot, a place where people sliced up whales in quite sickening ways. It was, as you might imagine, not a great boon for house prices: smell boiling blubber just once or twice, and death quickly loses its sting.

In 1831, then, Sydney's whaling station was moved to the other side of the harbour, and into the hands of one Archibald Mosman. His business was so successful he sold it just seven years later . . . because there were hardly any whales left.

MOUNT HOPE

From little things, big things grow, so long as the 'little thing' is something like coal. When a shepherd by the name of MacDowall discovered some of the black stuff on a New South Wales slope in 1873, he understandably got very excited, and gave said slope an appropriate name.

His excitement seemed to be very much justified in the days, years and decades that followed. At its peak, the bustling little town of Mount Hope had three mines and over 3000 residents.

Then it had a bushfire, and all hope was lost.

Nowadays, fewer than 20 people live in Mount Hope. And the only business in town is a pub.

MOUNT KOSCIUSZKO

Gough Whitlam is remembered for his commitment to many things, from education and health care to land rights and long conversations about Gough Whitlam.

But he should really be remembered for his commitment to spelling. The former prime minister spent more than 30 years pestering New South Wales bureaucrats to insert a 'z' into the spelling of 'Mount Kosciusko' until, in 1997, he finally met with success.

Whitlam's point was that the 'z' would have been there in the first place, only it somehow went missing. Kosciuszko was, after all, 'discovered' by a Polish explorer, and named after Tadeusz Kosciuszko, one of his nation's great heroes.

Or was it?

It turns out that Australia's highest mountain wasn't only missing a 'z' for some years, it was also missing k, o, s, c, i, u, s, k and o. The Mt Kosciuszko discovered by that Polish explorer is actually a few miles away from the mountain going by that name today.

According to the *Year Book Australia*, in 1910: 'Various measurements of the peak originally called by that name showed it to be slightly lower than its neighbour, Mount Townsend, and the names were thereupon transposed by the NSW Lands Department, so that Mount Kosciusko still remains the highest peak of Australia.'

MURRACOMPAGOORANDANNIE

'A person whose hand has been cut off.'

MUSCLE CREEK

Would you like to hear a tale about some hairy-shouldered hunk of testosterone who did something historical with his rippling biceps? A story about a modern-day Hercules or real-life Rambo, the sort of man's man who only ever stopped pumping iron in order to burp or take a couple of steroids?

Well, sorry, but you're out of luck. Muscle Creek in the Hunter Valley gets its name from its many *mussels*. It's just one of several New South Wales place names that some map or another once misspelled. What was wrong slowly became right, as the years trickled by . . . much like spending Friday and Saturday evenings on the couch, then turning in at nine o'clock for a good night's sleep.

Want more examples? I give you 'Coffs Harbour', which once was *Korff*'s Harbour, after a John Korff who sheltered there during a storm. Anna Bay, likewise, was once Hannah Bay, and Cherry Gully was Sherry Gully.

Antiene, while we're at it, ought to be Antrim (having been named after a county of that name in Ireland), and the Sydney suburb of Artarmon was named after Ardthelmon Castle (also in Ireland).

Okay, almost done. I just need to add that Morrisons Hill was named after a man named Morris, and Jewells after a Mr Jules.

MYSTERY BAY

Two mysteries surround Lamont H Young, a New South Wales surveyor from the 1870s. The first concerns his birth. Why on earth, once he was out of the womb, did his mum and dad decide to call him 'Lamont'?

The second mystery concerns his death. In October 1880, Young and four colleagues set sail from Bermagui in order to inspect a proposed site for a gold mine a few miles to the north. Three days later, their boat was discovered on a beach that we now call Mystery Bay. It contained five suitcases, all of Young's books and papers, plus some vomit, a bullet hole and a rock.

The boat didn't contain any of the men, however. And none of their bodies has ever been found.

NEVERTIRE

Try to discover the origins of the name 'Nevertire' and chances are you'll tire pretty soon.

As best as I can gauge, it came from the brother of one Henry Readford (a famous nighteenth-century cattle thief whose exploits inspired the novel *Robbery Under Arms*, about the bushranger Captain Starlight, written by Thomas Alexander Browne and published under the pseudonym Rolf Boldrewood). John Readford, on the other hand, was a legitimate cattle owner, though I'm guessing he liked to work his men hard. 'Nevertire' was the name of his cattle station.

The Warren Shire town was built much later, and for some reason borrowed the name.

NIMBIN

'A very small man.'

NO MISTAKE

A little north from what's now the little town of Parkes, a little gold was once dug up. 'There's more there, make no mistake,' someone supposedly said, and so gave a name to a brand new mine.

Humans *do*, however, make mistakes quite often, in large part because we are human. Sydney's Circular Quay, for example, is much more square-shaped than circular, and the suburb of East Hills is in Sydney's south-west.

Want one more? How about two? The village of Mount Hunter is quite a way away from any mountains, and the Sydney suburb of Five Dock is pretty light on for docks.

OMEGA

Driving through the suburbs is like sitting through a meeting, or trying to finish a Russian novel which resembles a brick. They just go on and on, and *on* and *on*, until time seems to come to a stop.

But it would be wrong to say that urban sprawl is the curse of the age (and not just because that honour goes to our shock jocks). Urban sprawl has been annoying people since long before we were all born.

If you get on to the Princes Highway, for example, and drive south from Sydney for about 100 years, you'll eventually pass the Omega Bridge. It got its name from a mansion that used to stand near there. Its owner figured that since it would *surely* be Sydney's most southerly settlement, it should be named after the last letter in the Greek alphabet.

Needless to say, he was wrong.

ORANGE

'Scotland' technically means 'land of the Irish', and one of the Beach Boys drowned. That is to say, not all names necessarily make a whole lot of sense.

Orange also belongs in this category, it being the centre of a fruit-growing region famous for its cherries, apples and pears. Oranges, however, are not grown in Orange (the climate being much too cool).

So what with the name, then? The answer lies with one Willem Frederick, a nineteenth-century Prince of Orange and self-proclaimed King of the Dutch. He fought (well, okay, watched) the Battle of Waterloo – and, while there, met Sir Thomas Mitchell, the starstruck soldier who would go on to become Surveyor-General of New South Wales and name a new town in his honour.

PACKSADDLE

If you were to chain a random stranger to a tree, and surgically remove both his or her feet, they would still be about as capable of exploring Australia as those two chumps Burke and Wills.

An ageing policeman and a just-qualified surveyor, with roughly zero days' exploring experience, Burke and Wills didn't just lose their lives in their 3000-kilometre hike through the desert, they also lost a great deal of luggage.

Generally, this was a bad thing. Such as when they lost a packsaddle in a creek north of Bathurst, where a small town of that name now stands.

But you'd have to suspect that sometimes they might have been secretly glad to lose an object or two. When Burke and Wills set off from Melbourne in 1860, they didn't just take enough food to last for two years. They also took several comfortable armchairs and a heavy oak table, plus a bathtub, a piano and a desk. Trees being so rare in Australia, they also took a few tonnes of firewood, and – just as importantly – lots of rockets and flags. All in all, their six wagons' worth of equipment weighed in at about 20 tonnes.

And that's not even counting the large Chinese gong.

PALM BEACH

Crystal-clear waters and wide turquoise skies. Bright golden sunshine and clean, crisp white sand. Such are the images evoked by the words 'Palm Beach', the Sydney suburb where *Home and Away* is filmed.

But would Palm Beach still be quite so attractive if it still had its original name? Once upon a time, you see, it was called 'Cranky Alice Beach', until some smart local sought out a change.

Smart locals, as it happens, have been at work all over Sydney: the city is chock-full of suburbs whose original names were, well, shit. Beverly Hills, for example, started out as 'Dumbleton', while Gladesville was once 'Doodys Bay'. Visitors to Orchard Hills were once visitors to 'Frogmore', and people from Eastlakes lived in 'Botany Swamps'.

And I think we can all agree that Rouchel sounds better than 'Ruck Hill', and Fairy Meadow more enticing than 'Cramsville'.

PEMULWUY

'Whatever anyone else could do, Pemulwuy did it better,' says the historian Eric Willmot. 'He could run further, he was one of the best. He could use a spear like no-one else could.'

And if you don't believe Willmot, you should ask Governor Phillip's gamekeeper. Only you can't, because Pemulwuy killed him with a spear. That incident, on 10 December 1790, was the start of this Indigenous warrior's 12-year war against the white settlers, a war which you'd have to say went pretty well.

Armed with just 'simple spears, rocks, boomerangs and stones, [Pemulwuy] defeated the British army', says another historian of another sortie. 'Every single soldier . . . that they sent in pursuit of Pemulwuy either walked back into the community with their saddle over their shoulders or they 'didn't make it back.'

Another famous battle saw him get shot seven times, in the head, limbs and chest, then taken to hospital in leg irons. He didn't just survive, he escaped within hours and fought on for another four years.

In the end, Pemulwuy's main enemy was overconfidence. 'After being wounded, all the people believed he was immune to British bullets. So he'd . . . stand right out in front of them and take them on, you know?'

Certainly a good story, but not such a great strategy: it turned out he wasn't actually immune at all.

PERISHER VALLEY

The importance of positive thinking is hard to overstate. Think happy thoughts and you'll feel happy feelings, even if everything around you more or less sucks.

It is a lesson that the good folks at Perisher might just profit from taking on board. Now the largest ski resort in the Southern Hemisphere, this New South Wales tourist Mecca might receive more tourists still if it didn't insist on continually reminding them that skiing carries the possibility of instant death.

The name supposedly comes from a nasty storm there that someone once sat through. 'What a perisher!' he apparently said (though we can't be sure, since that man is now dead).

POINT PIPER

Some people seem to think money is everything, but they forget that sex is important too. John Piper had plenty of both. A customs officer who 'collected' a great deal of tax, he had 18 children by five different women and several thousand acres all over Sydney.

But he was forced to sell just about all of them – including what's now Point Piper – after an official inquiry into his collecting methods forced him to abruptly resign.

'Some days before the news became public', it's said he 'hosted dinner for a few close friends. Midway through the party, he was rowed through Sydney Heads in his gig. He ordered his crew to play their instruments before throwing himself overboard. His crew heaved him back on board, unconscious but still very much alive.'

POISONED WATERHOLE CREEK

Racism can take many forms, some extremely subtle. Other forms, however, are not so subtle, such as poisoning an Aboriginal waterhole.

Such a homicide happened near Narrandera, and it happened simply because some white settlers wanted more land. After an unknown number of men, women and children were killed, the few surviving members of the tribe sought refuge in 'a densely timbered island in the Murrumbidgee River'.

But that didn't work out well either. It is now called Massacre Island.

PORT HACKING

It would be very easy to criticise Henry Hacking, so why don't we just go ahead and do that right now.

Best remembered for killing Pemulwuy, the Indigenous freedom fighter, this sailor-turned-convict-turned-bushman's career included convictions for perjury and theft, not to mention the attempted murder of his mistress.

'Useless as a (sea) Pilot from Drunkenness and other infirmities', Hacking was also not all that crash-hot on land, once mounting an expedition to cross the Blue Mountains, which turned back in less than a week.

But, hey – he 'discovered' Port Hacking. So please, people, don't be so picky.

PORT JACKSON

Technically speaking, there's no such thing as 'Sydney Harbour': its proper name is 'Port Jackson'.

But maybe it's appropriate no-one ever calls it that, for not even the man after whom it was named went by the name 'Jackson' for long.

A 'zealous friend' of Captain Cook and sometime lawyer for the Royal Navy, Sir George Jackson became Sir George Duckett later on in his life, under the terms of the will of his second wife's uncle.

POTTS POINT

As far as romance goes, Potts Point may disappoint: the Sydney suburb got its name from one of its first white residents . . . who was also the first ever employee at Westpac.

The suburb of Beecroft is perhaps a little bit more romantic, insofar as 'Beecroft' was the original surname of the first wife of the man who named it. Though, on the other hand, 'Beecroft' was also the name of his *second* wife, she being the first one's sister.

PRINCE ALFRED PARK

You could fill a book with the rules of royal protocol, and in fact, many people have. Male commoners must do a neck bow, female commoners a small curtsy. Touching a royal is a bit of a no-no, and one must always stand up when they enter a room, and not sit until they do.

And, just in case you were wondering, don't shoot them in the back.

It was this last piece of protocol that was, alas, breached when Queen Victoria's son visited the colonies in 1868. Though the young prince didn't die, and the would-be assassin was swiftly hanged, most Australians were a little embarrassed by the faux pas, and did what they could to make amends. The result was the Alfred Hospital in Melbourne and the Prince Alfred Hospital in Sydney – two buildings built via public subscription – plus the apologetic Prince Alfred Park.

PUNKALLY CREEK

'You are greedy.'

PUTTY

Putty, according to those in the know, is 'a generic term for material with a high plasticity, similar in texture to clay or dough'.

But do they also know it's the name of a town? Putty can be found not all that far from Singleton, if you travel north-west along the old Putty Road. Could the name date from when that road wasn't surfaced, and so soft it made travelling slow?

REIDS MISTAKE

Skill, smarts, strength, stamina: such qualities are simply vital when you're exploring unknown terrain.

Personally, however, I'd rather rely on luck. It certainly worked for Captain Bill Reid.

The 'discoverer' of Lake Macquarie became the discoverer of Lake Macquarie because navigation wasn't really his thing. Sent to fetch some coal from Port Hunter around 1800, Captain Reid took a few wrong turns, and then took about 18 more. He ended up in Australia's largest saltwater lake, the entrance to which now bears his name.

REPENTANCE CREEK

Long before road rage swamped our towns and cities, and caused the honking of a billion car horns, there was such a thing as *river rage* – and it could represent rather bad news for cows.

Repentance Creek got its name from a drover who flogged his bullock to death on its banks after it refused to follow him across. He 'then sat down by the waters and bitterly repented'.

ROBERTSON

There were a lot of things wrong with the twentieth century – genocide, war, environmental decay – but at least its politicians knew how to have a good time. From Stalin and Churchill to our own political boozehounds, alcoholics walked the corridors of power, and occasionally had a nap on the floor.

New South Wales's greatest statesman, at least in this one respect, was clearly Sir John Robertson. A five-time premier of the state, and the man after whom the Highlands village is named, he was said to have enjoyed a pint of rum in the morning, *every* morning, for over 35 years. 'None of the men who have left footprints in this country have been cold water men' ranks among his more memorable quotes.

THE ROCKS

Today's Australians tend to look on the convicts with what you might call a certain fondness. We see them as scallywags at worst and martyrs at best – as downtrodden, well-meaning, ill-treated types who just stole something minor, like a loaf of bread.

But the fact remains that they were, well, criminals, and thus often desperate or drunk. So common, in fact, were people who were 'on the rocks' in Sydney's early days, this may be the reason for the name of the suburb.

Or it could just be because there were a lot of rocks in The Rocks. Come to think of it, that sounds more likely.

ROOTY HILL

Opinion is divided when it comes to the name 'Rooty Hill' (though I think we can all agree it's not great).

One school of thought insists it's a reference to roti, that flat bread you use to scoop up your curry when you don't feel like naan bread or rice. There were plenty of Indians in the British Army, after all, and Rooty Hill's a place where a lot of wheat was once grown.

On the other hand, there's also a Rooty Hill on Norfolk Island. Could it have been named after that? So named because its roots were hard work to remove, Norfolk Island's Rooty

Hill was where a New South Wales governor lived before he came to Sydney and gave its version the name.

The third school of thought suggests that we stop thinking so much: could it simply be that Sydney's Rooty Hill once upon a time had a whole lot of roots. New South Wales is, after all, not exactly short on plainspoken place names. Take Big Springs, for example, which is not all that far from Black Swamp, or indeed Clear Creek, Dirty Creek and Dry Creek. The state also boasts a Dry Plain, a Green Valley, several Green Hills and a Rocky Glen.

And I'm not even going to mention High Range, Long Beach, Long Reef or Little River, let alone Red Hill, Rocky River, Round Mountain or Reedy Swamp. Oops – turns out I did.

ROSE BAY

No, this harbourside suburb was not named for its roses, but after an MP called Mr George Rose. Being British, he never went near the place, but presumably he knew someone who knew someone who did.

SURRY HILLS

It seems wrong to despise someone just because they can't spell, but to my mind it's as good a reason as any.

In the case of Sydney, however, I'm clearly going to need to make an exception to this rule, because what's wrong there can also be right. The suburb of Surry Hills, you see, was named after *Surrey* Hills in England, while Sutherland started out as *Southerland* (it being on the Georges River's south bank).

TAMBOURINE BAY

Playing the tambourine in public is a serious crime (or, at the very least, it probably should be). But it wasn't that which got Tambourine Nell into trouble.

A nineteenth-century Sydneysider 'of questionable repute', Nell made a living by day playing her tambourine in the streets, and by night as 'a notorious prostitute'. Her notoriety is said to have come from the way she tended to target sailors who had just come off a ship. 'She'd take them into the local pub, get them drunk and take them outside', then her 'mates would then roll them for their money.' The beauty of the plan was that they'd be back on their ships within days, and thus unable to help the police.

But even the best-laid plans can go wrong . . . Tambourine Bay marks the spot where Nell was eventually forced to hide out – until, alas, she was finally found.

Sydney

'Sydney' wasn't supposed to be the name of a penal colony – let alone the big city that it has since become. When the First Fleet set off in 1788, 'New South Wales' was the place that they sailed to. 'Sydney Cove' was just the name of a little cove (albeit the cove where they ended up landing).

What set Sydney Cove on the path to being a city was the fact that it wasn't much chop as a farm. Repeated crop failures eventually forced the colonists to look for more fertile pastures – which they eventually found in what's now Parramatta.

So in 1789, the colony of New South Wales was effectively split into two settlements – two settlements which it was often necessary to distinguish in conversation and letters back home. But since the more coastal 'Sydney' was the place that settlers sailed to and from, and the place where more of them were based, it slowly became shorthand for the colony itself. And in 1841, it became the official name when a new local government authority claimed formal jurisdiction over 'Sydney town'.

But where did the name 'Sydney' first spring from? The answer is Tommy Townshend. Made Baron Sydney of Chislehurst after the American War of Independence for his efforts to keep what's now Canada British, he was a cabinet minister who 'owed his political career to a very independent fortune . . . for his abilities, though respectable, scarcely rose above mediocrity.'

After that war ruled out the newly United States as a destination, it became Townshend's job to work out where to put England's criminals and, needless to say, he chose New South Wales.

He also personally selected Arthur Phillip to lead the First Fleet, and it's fair to say that Phillip was grateful. It was that 'talented but until then underrated officer' who sailed the fleet into Port Jackson – a place that Captain Cook had sailed past, and named, but not really explored – after the fleet's original destination of Botany Bay proved a bit of a dud. 'I fixed on a cove that had the best spring of water and in which the ships can anchor ... close to the shore,' Phillip wrote to his patron. 'This cove I honoured with the name of Sydney.'

And if you're wondering why Thomas Townshend chose the title 'Baron Sydney,' well, so are many of us. The answer is that he wanted to commemorate one of his ancestors, a Mr Algernon Sidney, who had been executed for questioning the divine right of kings.

But where did Algernon get the name? Well, one theory is that one of *his* ancestors had owned a place in Surrey called 'La Sydenye,' an Old English phrase meaning 'wide, well-watered land'.

But a better theory is that the family ultimately came from a French town called St Denis – which, in that language, sounds a bit like 'San Denny'. That town was in turn named after a famous Paris bishop, who had his head chopped off in what's now Montmartre ('the mountain of martyrs'). Undeterred, St Denis is said to have simply picked up his head and walked for six miles, while his mouth kept delivering a sermon.

Bondi Beach *From 'boondi', meaning 'water breaking over rocks'*
Castlereagh Street *Lord Castlereagh, Secretary of State for the Colonies, 1805–09*
Darling Harbour *Ralph Darling, NSW governor, 1825–31*
Elizabeth Street *Elizabeth Campbell, Governor Macquarie's second wife*
Fort Denison *Sir William Denison, NSW governor, 1855–61*
George Street *George III*
Hyde Park *After Hyde Park in London*
King Street *Philip Gidley King, NSW governor, 1800–06*
Luna Park *After Luna Park in New York's Coney Island*
Martin Place *Sir James Martin, NSW premier, 1863–65, 1866–68, 1870–72*
Oxford Street *After the London shopping strip*
Pitt Street *William Pitt the Younger, British Prime Minister, 1783–1801, 1804–06*
Taronga Zoo *An Indigenous word meaning 'beautiful view'*
Watsons Bay *After English sailor Robert Watson, an early settler*

TOM UGLYS POINT

I'm not, I think, an especially insecure person, but all in all my self-esteem is probably well-served by the fact that none of my nicknames seems to involve the word 'ugly'.

Thomas Huxley did not share my good fortune. This nine-teenth-century landowner owned what is now Tom Uglys Point, and acquired that nickname because no-one could quite pronounce 'Huxley'.

Or maybe not. Another theory is that the area was occu-pied by an entirely different Tom. *This* Tom really was ugly, alas, being a former soldier with only one eye.

ULTIMO

Lasting happiness is a hard thing to achieve; it's a recipe with a diverse range of ingredients. You need close friends and some kind of family, a fulfilling job and plenty of travel. Sex and alcohol are both crucial, of course, and I imagine that never meeting a tabloid journalist would also be a big help.

But one ingredient, I think, matters above all: everything else is icing atop this tasty cake. I am talking about the lasting joy that comes from some sort of bureaucratic error that ends up being to your benefit.

A Sydney surgeon of yesteryear knew this joy well. After 'falling foul' of the colony's police force in 1803, Dr John Harris received a summons to face a court martial, and braced himself for a stint in gaol.

But then he read the charge sheet more closely. It turned out he was formally charged with committing a crime on '19 ultimo' (or, in other words, the nineteenth of last month).

Since Dr Harris had actually committed his alleged crime on '19 *instant*' (the nineteenth of the *same* month), he was thus able to beat the charge with what you might call conspicuous ease.

To celebrate, he cheekily named his house 'Ultimo', and the suburb that grew around it eventually took that name too.

VAUCLUSE

The first man to build a mansion in Vaucluse, Sir Henry Brown Hayes, had a taste for all of life's finer things. You could tell this partly by the name he gave to his little palace, which eventually became the name of the area itself. Vaucluse House is named after Fontaine-de-Vaucluse, an elegant and ancient 'closed valley' in France.

But you could mainly tell by the way he kidnapped a wealthy heiress and pretended to marry her (with help from an accomplice who dressed up as a priest). That crime was the reason Sir Henry had come to Australia in the first place – he arrived as a convict in chains.

WAGGA WAGGA

Saying 'Wagga' just once seems weird enough, so why do we all then feel the need to repeat it?

The answer, my friends, is plurality. A 'wagga' is a crow, but Wagga Wagga has more than just one, which is why we need to say the word twice. 'Reduplication is often used as an intensifier' is how Wikipedia explains it, though to me that sentence doesn't explain much.

Anyway, these sorts of double-barrelled place names are far from unusual – and, to my mind, they all sound pretty fun. Among many, many other places, New South Wales can boast a Banda Banda, a Bong Bong, a Booti Booti and a Gumly Gumly: places which respectively contain 'many mountains', 'many watercourses', 'lots of things to eat' and 'plenty of frogs'.

WARDS MISTAKE

I may not have the makings of a master detective, or even a mid-level Scotland Yard bungler, but I *do* know that a man-hunt is more or less pointless if the man that you're hunting is in fact dead.

At least two cops, however, did not know this, if the story of Wards Mistake is not in fact a mistake.

The story goes that, two days after the killing of the 'gentleman bushranger' Frederick Ward, two troopers were attending a race meeting, when they noticed one of Ward's horses tied up at the track. After watching said horse for some time, they saw a man suddenly leap on it and gallop off as fast as he could.

The two troopers dutifully gave chase, before finally losing him at a stretch of land that's now 'Ward's Mistake'. It's so-called because, as they subsequently discovered, the rider could not have been Ward at all.

WARREN

It's hard to be certain how the town of Warren came to be, well, 'Warren' (though we shouldn't rule out the possibility that someone was having a laugh).

According to the *Sydney Morning Herald*, 'some say the name derives from a local Aboriginal word, meaning "strong" or "substantial". Another theory is that it represents the adoption of a contemporary English term, "warren", meaning a game park – perhaps a reference to the picturesque riverside setting . . . and the large numbers of wildlife in the area.'

Personally, I like to think that the town was settled by a bloke called Warren, perhaps with help from his mates, Shane, Trev and Bruce.

WATANOBBI

No, this Central Coast suburb was not named after some giant knob. Or, at least, there's no reason to think so. Historians have it that it's a reference to the hilliness (or, rather, the 'knobbiness') of the surrounding land.

WEE JASPER

This charmingly named town in New South Wales's Yass Valley was, alas, never home to a Jasper. Or, at least, not one who was associated with urine.

The name instead comes from a few little gemstones once found there by an anonymous Scotsman. They were a greenish, not-terribly-valuable variety of quartz which he proudly described as 'wee jaspers'.

WILLI WILLI NATIONAL PARK

'Evil spirits.' Make of that what you will.

WISEMANS FERRY

A nice little town on the Hawkesbury, Wisemans Ferry got its name from Solomon Wiseman, the former convict who ran its first ferry.

But if you think that having been a convict might have given him some sympathy for those who still were, you're going to need to think again. Fond of strutting about in a 'flowery vest, polished boots and dress sword', this self-proclaimed 'King of the Hawkesbury' would only ever employ convict labourers, and paid them with vicious beatings and terrible food. Many ended up trying to swim for their freedom, only to drown because he made them wear leg irons.

Other employees did not try to escape, but responded by working as well as they could. It's said that if Solomon really liked their work, he also liked to roundly abuse them just before their release. If the convict responded in kind, he 'would be lashed and his ticket of leave withheld for another year'.

WOMBAT

You'd think this little town would be named after a wombat, but I'm told you would be wrong. It was in fact named after wombat *poo*. When the explorers John Price and James Wilson named the area in 1798, their inspiration was apparently 'several sorts of dung of different animals', one of which – with that distinctive cube shape – they felt able to identify as a wombat's.

WOODBINE

People are a little precious about cigarettes these days (especially when you give one to their kids), but it was not always thus.

While the Sydney suburb of Woodbine was probably named after a local cottage, it's also said that, 'during a Council argument about the name of the suburb, a disgruntled councillor suggested it be named after the cigarettes of his chain-smoking colleagues, and it was from this off-the-cuff remark that serious consideration was given to the name Woodbine.'

Victoria

Dumpy, frumpy and faintly grumpy, Queen Victoria had protuberant eyes, a receding chin and an Empire Over Which The Sun Never Set. The ruler of a quarter of the globe for over six decades, the Great White Queen still seems to have about half of it named after her: there are Victoria streets, suburbs, parks, lakes and piers in close to 40 countries.

It was not, then, a terribly original move by Her Majesty in 1851 when she decided to lend her name to our newest colony. Australia may have already had a Great Victoria Desert, a Mount Victoria and a Victoria Pass (not to mention two Queenstowns and a couple of Queenscliffs), but why hide your light under a bushel when its bright rays bring so much warmth to the world?

Anyway, where were we? Oh, yes, the colony of Victoria – a colony which, from 1770 until 1851, had simply been a southern part of New South Wales. That name came from

Captain Cook, of course – as did Point Hicks, Cape Howe, Gabo Island and Ram Head, four places in today's state of Victoria that the *Endeavour* sailed by on its way to Botany Bay.

More explorers came by in the decades that followed – explorers later commemorated in towns like Bass and Flinders, plus the Hume Highway and Cape Schanck. They named Port Phillip Bay and King Island after New South Wales governors, and places like Cape Otway and Wilsons Promontory after obscure buddies back home. A ship called *Le Naturaliste* even visited the Île des Français, a place we now call French Island.

But it wasn't until the 1830s that the idea of settling the area was seriously explored. Whose idea it was remains a vexed question to this day: some people say John Batman, some say John Pascoe Fawkner. All we can say for a fact is that both of these Tasmanian businessmen identified the Yarra River as a good 'place for a village' and helped find people to live in it. Fawkner has been commemorated in the suburbs of Fawkner and Pascoe Vale, while Batman's wife and various business partners are remembered in place names like Mount Eliza, Swanston Street, Arthurs Creek, Mount Cottrell, Mount Connolly and the electorate of Gellibrand.

Batman himself, however, got nothing, unless you count two parks and a few little streets. An alcoholic who died young from syphilis, this was perhaps the price he paid for vaulting ambition: 'Batmania' had been his preferred name for the 'village', but it never quite took off.

Other names that were tossed around reportedly included Bearbrass, Birr-arrung, Bararing, Bareheap, Bareport, Barrern, Doutta Galla, Dutti-Galla, Glenelg and Phillip, but the 300 or so homes on the banks of the Yarra were mostly just known as 'the settlement'.

Or, rather, the illegal settlement. Technically speaking, the settlers were trespassing on Crown land, and New South Wales governor Richard Bourke told them as much. But in 1837, England's prime minister gave his blessing to the rapidly growing township – and thanks to Governor Bourke, he also gave it his name. Ordering his surveyor Robert Hoddle to lay out two towns, Bourke officially named the first town 'Melbourne' after that prime minister, Lord Melbourne, and the second one 'Williamstown', after William IV. He made sure that he too was remembered in the form of Bourke Street, while nearby Hoddle and Lonsdale streets memorialise two of his colleagues, and Elizabeth Street was named after his wife.

Later New South Wales governors got on the map too, of course – George Gipps with Gippsland; Charles Fitzroy with Fitzroy – and then when southern New South Wales became Victoria in 1851, the new colony's governors were happy to donate their names too. The Latrobe Valley, Mount Hotham, Canterbury and Loch all honour Brits who ended up in Government House.

Though the map also has plenty of Brits who stayed home. British royals, for example, are remembered in the Melbourne suburbs of Albert Park, Princes Hill and Brunswick, while Osborne, Sandringham and Windsor are all named after royal residences. Dukes are represented in Coburg and Portland, while if you want earls, barons or viscounts, I give you Mornington, Northcote, Castlemaine, Beaconsfield, Caulfield and Cranbourne.

Melbourne also isn't short on foreign place names, though by 'foreign' I mean English or Scottish. From Kensington to Keilor, something like half of all the suburbs in the city have a sort of cousin across the sea.

But as more and more settlers moved out of Melbourne, Indigenous names came into their own. From Warrnambool and Wangaratta to Moe and Mildura, it's thought that around 45 per cent of Victorian place names come from Wada Wurrung, Ngarigu and Gulidjan, to name just three of the state's 39 languages.

'I like the native names very much,' wrote one not un-typical settler in 1845. 'I think it a great pity to change them for English ones as it is often done.'

'The native appellations are far more characteristic and pleasing to the ear,' agreed someone else a decade later. 'Not that we condemn the application of her Majesty's name to this beautiful province but when scarcely a town, river or hill is found without some official's name, from the Premier down to the lowest clerk in the office, names that seldom possess euphony – the system is fulsome [that is, excessive].'

I'm not sure if Sir Richard Bourke would agree ...

A1

As towns go, A1 is a B2 at best. Little of it remains these days, thanks to bushfires, and its raison d'être, a gold mine, closed down many decades ago.

So what's with the name? It apparently comes from the gold that the mine *did* once produce. According to the mine

owners, it was pretty good stuff: pure, first class, crammed full of carats – or, as they put it, 'A1'.

ALBERT PARK

A year after her husband's death, Queen Victoria's children began to worry that she might end up going mad with grief.

Everybody else knew she already had. The clock on the Queen's bedroom was set to read 10.50 pm, 14 December 1861 – the moment that Prince Albert passed – and it stayed stuck on that time for the next two decades. Her dead husband's photo always lay on an empty pillow beside her, and she liked to keep a plaster cast of his hand within reach. Sorrow 'burns within me and wears me out!' Her Majesty wrote, from the cold, dark and remote Scottish castle where she started to spend all her time.

And it probably wore out most of her servants. They were all made to wear black every day for a year, and Victoria never wore any other colour again. Palace staff were ordered to maintain Albert's rooms exactly as he'd liked them, and to continue to bring in a bowl of hot water every morning, just as they always had, for his shave.

Next came a slew of public memorials – and I really do mean a slew. You can't throw a rock in the former British Empire without it landing somewhere near a place which the Queen said must be named after Albert.

ALBION

Long before Great Britain became Great Britain – or, if you'd prefer: England, Scotland and Wales – this rainy little island in the north-west of Europe was known to the ancients as 'Albion'. Since 'Alb' comes from the Latin 'albus', meaning 'white', it was probably a reference to the White Cliffs of Dover, but we're unlikely to ever know for sure.

What we *do* know for a fact is that for a certain sort of Australian, any and all immigration will always signal the end of the world. While these days it's Middle Eastern people who are 'ruining our culture' and 'taking our jobs', it was 'the Asians' back in the '80s, and in the '40s, the Italians and Greeks.

In the 1840s, however, it was the Irish. They were 'liars' and 'dirty' and 'not quite human'. And, being Catholic, they were heretics too.

And thus it was that when some 'real' Australians settled a suburb in Melbourne's west, they naturally stipulated that only pure-blooded Britons could live there. To make that extra clear to the sub-human heretics, they called it 'Albion'.

ANGLESEA

The gateway to the Great Ocean Road, Anglesea on Victoria's Surf Coast is a magnet for tourists in summer.

But would they all come in such big numbers if it was still called 'Swampy Creek'?

BACCHUS MARSH

Bacchus was the Roman god of wine. Fond of getting completely shit-faced, he was a young, sensuous and 'womanish' deity who liked to strut about naked with ithyphallic satyrs (ithyphallic satyrs being goat-men with giant stiffies). His other hobbies included holding a pine cone a lot, but this is a technicality which need not concern us here.

The point is, none of these hobbies is really something most of us associate with Bacchus Marsh. And in this, we are all quite correct. The town was founded by one William Bacchus, who as far as I know got about fully clothed.

BADDAGINNIE

Always pay your workers, or at the very least give them food. Whoever was in charge of building the Baddaginnie railway station seems to have forgotten this, and his Sri Lankan labourers didn't suffer in silence. 'Baddaginnie' is a Sinhalese expression that means something like 'empty belly'.

BADGER CREEK

There are no badgers in Badgers Creek, but there may still be a Badger. Or at least what remains of his bones. The name comes from a carthorse who couldn't really swim.

BALACLAVA

The suburb of Balaclava was named after a Black Sea port where shots were fired during the Crimean War. Best remembered for the Charge of the Light Brigade ('Theirs not to reason why; theirs but to do and die'), the Battle of Balaclava is also famous for its contributions to fashion.

To combat the cold Russian winters, some British troops wore these woolly hats, which they called 'balaclavas'. Lord Cardigan's regiment, on the other hand, were given a sort of buttoned-up woollen vest.

BALWYN

Until its residents finally came to their senses in 2009, the leafy Melbourne suburb of Balwyn spent 81 years as an alcohol-free zone. With no pubs, no bars and no wine in its restaurants, the people of Balwyn basically spent the best part of a century with no real reason to live.

Ironic, in a way, as it began life as a vineyard. A combination of Saxon and Gaelic, 'Bal-wyn' means 'home of the vine'.

BASS

A crewmate of Matthew Flinders as he charted the Australian coast, George Bass is all over the map these days. Along with the little town of Bass, there's a Bass Hill, a Bass Point and a Bass River, two Bass highways and, of course, the Bass Strait.

But where is Bass himself? That's the question a lot of people were asking themselves when George set off from Sydney to South America in 1803 . . . and was never seen again. One account has it that he was caught trying to sell (or rather smuggle) something illegal there, and was either shot or sent to the silver mines. But if so, what happened to his ship? Or, indeed, its 25-man crew?

Chances are that they simply sank somewhere, but that we'll never know for sure.

BENDIGO

Some people say that Bendigo was named after Abednego Thompson. The 'Champion Prize Fighter of All England' at a time when boxing was illegal and no-one wore gloves, 'Bendigo' was a fast-moving, balletic southpaw who had a big fan base all over the world.

But I'm here to tell you that these people are wrong. Yep, that's right: wrong. The Victorian gold rush town was actually named after an *Australian* bare-knuckle boxer, who got his nickname from 'Bendigo' Thompson. Being slower and somewhat less balletic than the English version, *our* boxer spent most of his career as a shepherd, in the fields where the town stands today.

BIG HILL

Victoria's settlers were a sturdy breed, with no time for flim-flam or flummery. The state thus boasts no less than six 'Big Hills', plus Big Desert, Big Lake and a Big River.

BONNIE DOON

'Aft hae I rov'd by Bonie Doon, to see the rose and woodbine twine. And ilka bird sang o' its Luve, and fondly sae did I o' mine.'

Did that make any sense to you? Don't worry, I was struggling too.

All you really need to know is that it's part of a poem by Robbie Burns. It commemorates 'ye banks and braes o' bonnie Doon,' which I believe is a Scottish river. At least one white settler must have known for sure, since he used the phrase for his parcel of land.

BOOMAHNOOMOONAH

'Good prose is like a windowpane,' as George Orwell once put it: simple to read, easy to say, and above all, crystal clear. A good writer makes things snappy. His or her sentences soar off the page.

I feel that George wouldn't approve of my next paragraph, but what the hell, let's push on. Victoria has a number of long and unpronounceable place names which I feel are worth mentioning, and which I would like you to now read out loud.

Ready? Then here we go: Tarrayoukyan, Thologolong, Wallangaraugh, Korweinguboora, Kooroocheang, Warracknabeal, Watchegatchwca, Tichingorourke, Upotipotpon, Waggarandall, Waanyarra, Woohlpooer, Carraragarmungee, Wulgulmerang, Mollongghip, Nyerimilang, Patchewollock, Boomahnoomoonah, Naringaninga, Gringegalgona, Connewirrecoo, Dooboobetic, Duchembegarra, Pannoobamawm, Korweinguboora, Kinimakatka, Whanregarwen and Wondoomarook.

How did you go?

BRUNSWICK

In 1795, England's Prince of Wales was not so much a prince as a mountain of debt. Marriage was the only possible way in which he could pay off his creditors, and his wealthy German cousin, Caroline of Brunswick, seemed like the only possible choice. The two had never met before, and were not at all keen to do so now, but duty called, parents insisted, and a date was duly set.

Three days before the ceremony, the prince met his fiancée for the first time – and a close observer may have been able to tell he wasn't too pleased. 'Harris, I am not very well, pray get me a glass of brandy,' were Prince George's first words after setting eyes on his 'short, fat and ugly bride' – a woman whose 'body odour was overwhelming' as she 'never changed her undergarments, and rarely washed'.

George continued to drink brandy until the morning of the wedding, and was said to be so drunk on their wedding night that he fell asleep in the fireplace.

Disgust steadily grew into hatred and when the prince became king, he tried to secure a divorce. Many people, however, were outraged at this, and campaigned on the queen's behalf. One such person was Thomas Wilkinson, a Victorian landowner, who named some of his land after her home.

BRUTHEN

'Place of evil spirits.'

BUMBANG ISLAND

Not so much as 'island' as a leafy bend in the Murray, Bumbang Island has a name to remember – though when it comes to exactly what it means, we've apparently all forgotten.

BUNYIP

Did a bunyip ever live in Bunyip?

No, but a diprotodon might have. A sort of 2-metre-tall, 3-metre-long wombat, with protruding teeth and gigantic claws, this ancient marsupial was still around 60 000 years ago, when the first citizens arrived on our shores. For palaeontologist Patricia Vickers-Rich, Indigenous legends like the bunyip 'perhaps stem from an acquaintance with prehistoric bones or even living prehistoric animals themselves ... When confronted with the remains of some of the now extinct Australian marsupials,' she says, Aborigines 'often identify them as the bunyip'.

CAPE CLEAR

A 'cape' is another name for headland – that is, a bit of coast that juts out into the sea. So it's not, all things considered, the most obvious term to apply to a town that's 100 kilometres inland. Cape Clear's name is said to come from a prominent sign that someone once put by a boggy road. It was apparently supposed to read '*Keep* Clear', but good intentions don't always lead to good spelling.

CARLTON

The Carlton House set: boasting strange names like Lord Manners and 'Poodle' Byng, they were 'a glitzy mixed bag of effétes, fops, rakes, rogues, scholars, gamblers and duchesses' who liked to party at Carlton House, the home of Prince George.

Weighing in at around 20 stone (127 kilograms), the 'Prince of Whales' was often accused of spending all his time drinking and gambling, but this was unfair, because he also liked to have sex.

'The bacchanalian orgies of Carlton House were . . . of a most extraordinary description,' wrote one correspondent of 'that royal brothel', which later lent its name to a Melbourne suburb. 'The dances which were exhibited for the amusement of the companions of the prince were performed by females whose sole aim and study appeared to have been, like the dancing girls of the East, to perfect themselves in voluptuousness of attitude, and in a shameless exposure of their person, to the unrestrained gaze of the libidinous voluptuary.'

All in all, the house more closely resembled 'the interior of a Turkish seraglio, than the abode of a British Prince'.

CHADSTONE

We all get annoyed with our kids at times, but murder may be an overreaction.

King Wulf didn't agree. That seventh-century ruler of Mercia killed his two sons in a fit of rage. But to be fair, we should note that he felt a certain amount of remorse, and so went to his bishop to try to atone.

Bishop Chad basically said don't sweat it, for God forgives all sins, but it might help move things along a bit if you build a church. So King Wulf promptly did just that, building a big edifice that became known as 'Chad's stone'.

Over 1300 years later, some Melbourne developers stole the name, and proceeded to build an edifice of their own. Chadstone is now one of the world's biggest shopping malls. I rather doubt that God forgave *them*.

CHINKAPOOK

No-one quite knows what a 'chinkapook' is, but there's every chance that it's a foot.

CHUM CREEK

Being a chum is fun,
that is why I'm one.

That 1930s classic, just to be clear, has nothing whatsoever to do with Chum Creek. Perhaps this would have been clearer if I hadn't referred to the song, but I guess now we'll never know.

Chum Creek's name comes from the fact that it was once a gold mine with an unusually large number of inexperienced diggers, or 'new chums', as they were known in the trade.

CHURCHILL

After World War II was won, and western civilisation made safe for all, there was some talk of renaming the Northern Territory after Sir Winston Churchill.

Most people said 'Shut up', however, and instead gave his name to a tiny town. Previously known as 'Hazelwood', Churchill mostly houses employees of what used to be the State Electricity Commission and is every bit as small and dull as it sounds.

COLLINGWOOD

'You are trapped in a room with a crocodile, a cobra and a Collingwood fan. You have a gun with two bullets. What do you do?'

The answer is, of course, 'shoot the Collingwood fan twice'. Much like some politicians and whoever happens to be the latest reality TV star, Collingwood fans belong in the category of people we love to hate.

It's a state of affairs that would sadden Vice-Admiral Cuthbert Collingwood, the man after whom the suburb was named. A hero of the Battle of Trafalgar, Collingwood is mainly remembered for having been a nice person at a time when most sea captains only emerged from their cabins to flog someone or order a hanging.

'A better friend to seamen never trod the quarterdeck,' wrote one contemporary. 'He and his dog Bounce were known to every member of the crew. How attentive he was to the health and comfort and happiness of his crew! A man who could not be happy under him, could have been happy nowhere.'

DEAD HORSE HILL

All types of people came to Victoria during the gold rush, not just the sort of men who think cowpoke's a verb. Every week would see another ship arrive from Europe or California or China and disgorge another army of optimistic souls. Clerks, cobblers, chemists, couriers: all, for a time, became gold miners, and helped to lend the profession a certain *je ne sais quoi*. With high hopes and horribly low skill levels, together with some bad maps and overpriced tools, they created boom towns out of the badlands, turning tents into permanent buildings, and bushland into shops, parks and pubs.

But let's not forget that lots of animals came too. And by and large, they didn't have a good time. Littered, as they were, with pits, mounds and ridges, Victoria's gold fields included such places as Dead Dog Gully, Pig Face Gully, Dead Horse Flat and Dead Bullock Creek.

DEAD MANS GULLY

Building a railway line is a dangerous business (and I suspect quite a dull one as well). Proof of this came in 1877, at what's now called Dead Mans Gully, when a worker named John Mollison was accidentally killed by a wayward shaft. For whatever reason, he was buried right there and then, in a grandiose grave just beside the road.

According to Annie O'Reilly, the brains behind the Odd History blog, the piece of road that ran by the grave later became a notorious black spot. 'There were numerous deaths and injuries between 1889 and 1929,' and in most cases a cause could not be determined.

DEVILS RIVER

I've been told that I'm a bad singer by a quite a few people – among them, alas, my mum. But I'd like to point out that my voice has never once been mistaken for Satan's, which may be all the encouragement I need to sing on.

Some Indigenous folk were less fortunate in this respect. Devils River received its dark name after some settlers overheard a corroboree.

DIGGERS REST

A resting place on the road to the gold fields. Having driven through it once or twice, I wouldn't suggest that you linger today.

DOGS GRAVE

'If I have any beliefs about immortality,' James Thurber once remarked, 'it is that certain dogs I have known will go to heaven, and very, very few persons.'

For Boney's sake, let's hope that he's right. Dogs Grave gets its name from a cattle dog whose owner set a trap for some dingos one night. But it was Boney who managed to fall into it. Devouring the strychnine-laced bait, he was dead by the next day.

Traumatised, his owner erected a grave, and a version of it still stands to this day.

EL DORADO

Is it possible to see into the future?

Maybe, if your name's William Baker. A captain in the Royal Navy, Baker became a cattle farmer in 1840, after buying a small plot of land. He named it 'El Dorado', after South America's mythical city of gold.

Twelve years later, gold was discovered nearby, and El Dorado became a gold rush town.

EMERALD CREEK

There are no emeralds in Emerald Creek, I'm afraid, but if you look closely, you might find a corpse. Now the name of the suburb that surrounds it, the creek got its name from the unfortunate Jack Emerald, a miner who was murdered on its banks.

Similar disappointment awaits visitors to Diamond Creek, a suburb 80 kilometres to Emerald Creek's north. 'Diamond' wasn't a diamond – he was a bull who somehow managed to drown.

ENDEAVOUR HILLS

From Van Gogh and Gauguin to my four-year-old self, quite a few of history's greatest artists weren't really appreciated in their own time.

The same could be said for some ships. An 'ugly and awkward little vessel' that spent most of its career carrying cargoes of coal, the HMS *Endeavour* is today celebrated all over the world. It's lent its name to suburbs and rivers, inlets and islands, big and small ships and a massive space shuttle.

A vessel that, as Captain James Cook put it, 'sailed further than any man has been before', the *Endeavour* is even thought to have inspired Star Trek's USS *Enterprise* (a vessel under the command of Captain James *Kirk* that set out 'to boldly go where no man has gone before').

But that is now. What about *then*? It's worth remembering that after the *Endeavour* finished its epic three-year voyage to Australia, it spent the next few years transporting rope and tar. Then when the American colonies decided that they wanted independence, the ship was sent to Rhode Island and deliberately sunk, as part of an effort to blockade a port.

It's still there, somewhere under the ocean, no doubt feeling slightly miffed.

EUREKA

If you've ever wondered what 'eureka' means, I can reveal that it's the first person singular perfect indicative active form of the verb εὑρίσκω (*heuriskō*). Does that clear matters up?

No?

Sigh. Eye roll. Okay, then: I can also reveal that it's a phrase from ancient Greece that means something along the lines of 'I found it'. And thus not a bad name for a gold mine.

FITZROY

Melbourne's funkiest suburb gets its name from the not-terribly-funky Sir Charles Augustus Fitzroy, New South Wales's governor in the late 1840s. Educated at Harrow and impeccably well-table-mannered, he was related to the dukes of Grafton, a former prime minister, and Charles Darwin's captain aboard the *Beagle*.

But his most interesting ancestor would be Henry Fitzroy, the illegitimate child of Charles II. 'Fitzroy' means 'son of royalty'.

GABO ISLAND

The Gabo Island story tends to go as follows: an explorer (usually Captain Cook) once asked an Indigenous man, 'What is this island's name?' His answer was 'Gabo', meaning 'I don't understand', and 'Gabo' the name thus became.

GENTLE ANNIE

A somewhat windy stretch of land near Whitfield, Gentle Annie probably gets its name from a Scottish weather spirit who was not really gentle at all. Responsible for south-westerly gales in the Highlands, she was a one-eyed 'hag' with blue, scaly skin who it was best not to offend, lest she start to blow. Her touchiness was associated with treachery, not to mention 'cold, dissolution and death'.

Or maybe not. While we know that Victoria's Gentle Annie was settled by a Scotsman, whether he had some ancient legend in mind is really anyone's guess.

JOLIMONT

Home to the hallowed turf of the MCG, the suburb of Jolimont is not described as 'a pretty mountain' all that often. But that – in French – is what Governor La Trobe decided to call it, because 'Jolimont' was the name of his Swiss wife's home.

KATAMATITE

A little town 50 kilometres north of Shepparton, Katamatite is probably a corruption of 'Catamateet', the Indigenous name for a nearby creek.

But let's not rule out the possibility that it comes from 'catamite', the Ancient Greek term for a comely young boy who was the 'intimate companion' of an older man.

KERANG

No-one can quite agree what Kerang means. My favourite option is 'parasite', though 'edible root vegetable' also has its charms.

KINGLAKE

The town of Kinglake hit the headlines in 2009, and no doubt caused plenty of tears. For it was there that Black Saturday burnt its fiercest, killing 38 people and devouring around 500 homes.

But amid all the sadness and heartache, there must have been at least one or two people scratching their heads. I mean, what about the *lake*, for God's sake? Why on earth didn't people just go there?

The short answer is that there *is* no lake. Dryer than a dead dingo's donger, the bushfire-prone town was named after Alexander Kinglake, a British historian who died at age 32 after writing the definitive account of the Crimean War.

KOROIT

Some Indigenous words are *seriously* ancient – and if you have any doubt, I present the town of Koroit. About 180 kilometres west of Melbourne, it is 'one of Australia's foremost potato producers', thanks to its rich and fertile black soil.

That fertility didn't just happen, however. It comes from the fact that there is a (now-extinct) volcano nearby.

Many people have argued that the name also comes from the volcano. But if 'koroit' does indeed mean 'fire', as the theory goes, then it's reasonable to assume that it's been around for a while. The volcano's most recent eruption was 6000 years ago.

LEONGATHA

'Teeth.'

LILLIPUT

Ruled over by the Emperor Golbasto Momarem Evlame Gurdilo Shefin Mully Ully Gue, the residents of Lilliput don't weigh much and tend to be about 6 inches (15 centimetres) tall. Violent, mean and strangely dressed, they have strong views about rope dancing and frequently wage war over the subject of eggs.

I am, of course, talking about the Lilliput in *Gulliver's Travels*: a tiny island of tiny people with tiny and vicious minds. The Victorian region that adopted its name probably did so at the behest of a cattle farmer whose surname was the similar 'Gullifer'.

It's worth noting, however, that the *fictional* Lilliput is also in Australia, if we take the broad view. Published in 1726, *Gulliver's Travels* includes pseudo-coordinates for Lilliput which place it a bit west of Tasmania.

LITTLE DONKEY WOMAN SWAMP

No idea, sorry. Suggestions welcome.

MIEPOLL

According to Bill Beatty's *Treasury of Australian Folk Tales* (which may not be a title that inspires total confidence), the farming district of Miepoll took its name from a magistrate who was eager to please. A slave to public opinion, whatever the public's opinion might happen to be, he is said to have prefaced all of his judgements with the phrase 'My poll says . . .'.

MOE

'Swampland.'

MONKEY GULLY

The story goes that a monkey once hid here after making its escape from a travelling circus.

And the story is, of course, false. If someone did see a 'monkey' here, what they really saw would have been a koala.

MOUNT BLOWHARD

Sigmund Freud was the sort of person who saw sex wherever he looked. Anything long and pointy was clearly a penis; anything that was round represented a boob. A vagina was basically any sort of passageway, while if you've ever had a dream about climbing some stairs, what you *really* dreamed about was having a wank.

It's fairly easy to imagine what Freud would have made of Mount Blowhard, a windy hill in Victoria's east.

MOUNT BOGONG

'Infested with flies.'

MOUNT BOOBYALLA

Sorry, lads: a boobyalla is a type of shrub.

MOUNT BUGGERY

When that nun from *The Sound of Music* urges Maria to 'climb every mountain', she is clearly speaking as a person who had never climbed 'Crosscut Saw'.

As a hiker who *has* climbed this range, I can report that it's a bad idea. You go up a big mountain, pant for while, then clamber down it, and collapse for a bit. After you've checked your pulse, and shed a few tears, this process is repeated, again and again. The final treat is a *really big* mountain, at which point you start to pray for sweet death.

Melbourne

Melbourne gets its name from Lord Melbourne, Britain's prime minister back in 1836, when a small village was founded on the banks of the Yarra.

A student companion of Byron and Shelley – and bed companion of practically everyone else – Melbourne was what you might call an old-style aristocrat. Urbane, insouciant and possessed of dashing grey side whiskers, he was of a generation that drank port for breakfast, and did something scandalous at least twice before lunch. He came from an age of powdered wigs and heavy bosoms; an age of idlers and gamers, and rogues and rakes, and dandies and wenches and bucks. Fond of 'spanking sessions with aristocratic ladies', and known to whip 'orphan girls taken into his household as objects of charity', what Lord Melbourne didn't know about sex was not worth knowing – though he still would have been prepared to give it a go.

And he was also what you might call lazy. A man who became prime minister by accident, and found policy-making a bit of a bore, Melbourne's most famous achievement was essentially achieving nothing at all. His Lordship didn't just take a hands-off approach to the prime ministership; he also closed his eyes and blocked his ears. 'Why not leave it alone?' tended to be his response whenever anyone asked him to do, well, anything.

But did he leave the young Queen Victoria alone? While they were 40 years apart in age, the young monarch and her prime minister were very often together. She spent over six hours a day in his company, as a teenager: riding and dining, playing chess and charades, and chatting about everything under the sun. He went with her on daily walks in the park, and graced her dinner table most nights of the week. He even got his own apartment at Windsor Castle . . .

Bourke Street   *Sir Richard Bourke, NSW governor, 1831–37*

Collins Street   *David Collins, Lieutenant-Governor of Van Diemen's Land, 1804–10.*

Elizabeth Street   *Bourke's wife*

Hoddle Street   *Robert Hoddle, designer of the CBD grid*

King Street   *Philip Gidley King, NSW governor, 1800–06*

La Trobe Street   *Charles La Trobe, Lieutenant-Governor of Victoria, 1851–54*

Lonsdale Street   *Captain William Lonsdale, colonial administrator, 1840s*

Punt Road   *Named after a punt that used to carry passengers across the Yarra*

Queen Street   *Queen Adelaide, William's wife*

Russell Street   *Lord John Russell, British prime minister, 1846–52*

Spencer Street   *Lord John Spencer, Chancellor of the Exchequer, 1834–37*

Spring Street   *Thomas Spring Rice, Chancellor of the Exchequer, 1835–39*

Swanston Street   *Captain Charles Swanston, financier, 1830s to 1840s*

William Street   *William IV*

The first men to do this foolish thing were members of the Melbourne Walking Club, back in the '30s. It's said that one of them had just about reached journey's end when he discovered the special treat at the end of the Saw.

'What? Another bugger?' he panted. 'I'll call this mountain Mt Buggery.'

MOUNT LITTLE DICK

Not all that far from Ramrod Creek (not to mention the splendidly named Spanker Knob) lies a proud edifice called Mount Little Dick. Did a small man named Richard once live there? Let's all just hope for the best.

MOUNT MACEDON

The son of Macedonia's Phillip II, Alexander the Great essentially conquered Greece by the time he was 20, then quickly knocked over the Middle East. He also managed to shack up with a eunuch and drink himself to death before he even hit his mid-30s.

Achievements like this tend to stick in the mind. Or at least they do if you're Sir Thomas Mitchell. When that nineteenth-century explorer reached the top of a hill near Woodend, he found he could see all the way to Port Phillip Bay, some 70 kilometres to the south. While that bay had been named after Governor Arthur Phillip, seeing it made Mitchell think of Phillip II – and so he named the hill 'Mount Macedon'.

A theme having thus been established in his mind, Mitchell went on to name another hill Mount Alexander, and the Campaspe River after Alex's concubine.

MOUNT TERRIBLE

'If you don't have a mountain, build one and then climb it,' says that well-known philosopher Sylvester Stallone. 'And after you climb it, build another one. Otherwise, you start to flat-line in your life.'

The first white settlers had plenty of mountains to climb, but from the sound of things, they'd have been better off flatlining. Victoria boasts a Mount Terrible and a Mount Disappointment, a Mount Despair and a Mount Hopeless.

You can also climb Mount Fainter or stagger up the Devils Staircase -- a summit from which it's possible to see Hells Window and Horrible Gap.

MURDERING GULLY

'I am innocent of any improper treatment of the aboriginal natives of this district,' wrote Frederick Taylor, a nineteenth-century sheep farmer, to Victoria's Governor La Trobe.

After reviewing the 'evidence', La Trobe agreed, and let Frederick Taylor buy a few more farms.

This evidence, in case you were wondering, was a state-ment from one of Taylor's employees to the effect that he may have seen an unidentified Aborigine killing an unidentified sheep at an unidentified point in time. Taylor's response was to visit a random Indigenous settlement, open fire, and kill 35 adults and kids.

OZENKADNOOK

'Very fat kangaroo.'

PETTICOAT CREEK

One or two daughters is obviously a blessing, but eight sounds a bit like a curse.

We should, then, pity poor Henry Biddle. A nineteenth-century settler with a home near Colac, that father had eight daughters to feed. It's said that the family's washing line could be seen from far away, and that it was generally heaving with petticoats.

POINT HICKS

When the *Endeavour* sailed within sight of Australia on 20 April 1770, Captain Cook wasn't the first to see it. The honour of shouting 'Land ahoy!' went to a lieutenant named Zachary Hicks.

To this day, no-one's quite sure which particular bit of land Hicks saw, of all the options on Victoria's north coast. But the best guess is a cliff that juts out of east Gippsland – and that's why we call it Point Hicks.

POOWONG

Not a great name for a town, all up, and the meaning makes it even worse. 'Poowong' is thought to mean 'carrion' (that is, a decaying corpse).

PORT FAIRY

No fairies ever came to Port Fairy, I'm afraid, just a ship filled with blubber and blood. The coastal town was named after a whaling ship called the *Fairy* which sailed past in 1828.

PRETTY SALLY HILL

A dormant volcano in the Great Dividing Range, Pretty Sally Hill was once home to a pretty seedy pub.

Operating without a liquor licence, or all that much in the way of good hygiene, the illegal shanty was run by one 'Pretty Sally,' a woman who was 'pretty' in the same way that Donald Trump is likeable and possessed of great charm and good taste. 'Brim-full of fun and laughter', she was 'a very stout and ugly old woman' who weighed in at 22 stone.

According to an 1861 travel book, Sally died as a result of drink-driving, when her horse and cart crashed into a stump. 'My word, sir,' a witness supposedly said, 'had you seen that overgrown huge mountain of flesh fall from the dray, and roll over and over, you never would have forgotten it. The earth fairly shook from violent concussion.'

ROSEBUD

History is full of steady, reliable ships that sailed here and there without a hitch, carrying cargoes of this and that.

Geography, however, rarely mentions them. If you're a ship and you want to get on a map, I advise you to get stuck on a sandbar, ideally one close to the shore.

Such was the fate of the *Rosebud*, a boat that was filled with household goods, but light on for a crew that could sail. As it mouldered near a beach on the Mornington Peninsula, that beach became known as the Rosebud beach – and so too did the surrounding suburb.

SAFETY BEACH

Safety Beach is a good example of what happens when you get a bunch of savvy marketing types together and for some reason fail to shoot them.

Originally called 'Shark Bay', for the very good reason that it was prone to sharks, it became Safety Beach after nearby towns such as Sorrento started to become popular with tourists.

To reinforce the point that Shark Bay was now 'safe', a local landowner organised a shark cull. Seven big toothy corpses were then stuck on poles on the beach, which I suspect probably didn't help.

ST KILDA

Catholic saints are a strange old bunch. For every one of them doing something sensible, like slaying a dragon or speaking in tongues, there's someone like St Joseph, who spontaneously levitates, or St Agatha, who cut off her breasts. My personal favourite is St Denis, who walked around without his head, but he's only just ahead of St Simeon, who lived on a pole.

There are no stories about St *Kilda*, however, because he or she doesn't exist. The Melbourne beachside suburb was named after a ship called the *Lady of St Kilda*, which moored there in the 1840s.

That ship, in turn, was named after a small Scottish island (where a Lady Grange was imprisoned years ago). No-one quite knows how the island became 'St Kilda', but the best guess is that it's a corruption of 'sunt kelda', a Viking phrase meaning 'sweet well water'.

SEA LAKE

Now I may not be an oceanographer, but it seems to me that there's something slightly odd about calling some water 'Sea Lake'.

And it turns out that I'm right. 'It is purported that a surveyor mistook a mark on hand drawings "see lake" which had been used by the author of the drawings to mark a landmark.'

SHAG ISLAND

A shag is a species of cormorant (that is, an aquatic bird). There are probably quite a few of them at Shag Island, near Wilsons Promontory, and that's presumably why it got the name. But at this early stage of our investigation, let's not rule other explanations out.

SMELLIE INLET

Not actually all that smelly, unless you strongly object to seaweed, this little inlet on the south-east coast was apparently settled by a Mr James Smellie.

SMOKO

The tradition of the smoko probably began in the British Navy, but Australian sheep shearers quickly got in on the act. Now a little hamlet in the High Country, Smoko started out as a sheep station where, from the sound of things, not much got done.

SNOBS CREEK

You'd think that no true snob would have gone near Australia, back in the day, let alone got snooty about one of its creeks.

Surely they'd be too busy hunting foxes, while their kids got molested at boarding school?

Nope. Colonial Australia was actually *crawling* with snobs, because that word also used to mean 'bootmaker'. One such artisan clearly lived in Snobs Creek.

SPANKER KNOB

When a small bushfire broke out in Victoria in 2012, one or two reports in a few local papers soon led to headlines all over the world. This was not, alas, out of any great concern for our welfare, but because the fire had been lit at a hill with a slightly odd name.

Who the hell named 'Spanker Knob' remains a mystery to this day, but the name seems to post-date the nearby 'Spanker Road'. One theory is that it was considered to have been 'a spanker of a run' – that is, a nice, easy drive.

SUGGAN BUGGAN

A (slightly odd) riff on 'bukkan bukkan', an Indigenous phrase meaning 'bags made from grass'.

SUNSHINE

No, this suburb in Melbourne's west was not named for its unusually fine weather and abundance of natural light. It was named after a massive grey factory that was owned by the Sunshine Harvester Works.

TINAMBA

'Pull my toe.'

TITTYBONG

Possibly the best-named town in all Australia, if not the western world, Tittybong is a bit of a mystery. We don't know where the name comes from. All we know is that it is good.

THE TWELVE APOSTLES

While Jesus had no less than twelve apostles, Victoria has just eight. The scattered remains of an eroded coastline, these eight big hunks of limestone near the Great Ocean Road have long been a drawcard for tourists.

But would they be so keen to see the Twelve Apostles, I wonder, if they were still called 'the Sow and Piglets'?

VITE VITE

Meaning, as it does, 'quick quick' in French, Vite Vite sounds like a place people are quite keen to leave. The name is thought to come from some railway passengers who were keenly awaiting their train.

WARRNAMBOOL

Not only is Warrnambool not in Warrnambool, its name should really be Wheringkernitch.

Can we end things there, or do I need to elaborate?

On reflection, perhaps this would be best. The theory goes that when white settlers arrived in what's now Warrnambool, they asked a local Aborigine for the district's name,

The problem, however, was that the Aborigine *wasn't* a local, and he thought they were asking him *where he came from.* 'Warrnambool,' he therefore replied, referring to a mountain about 10 kilometres away.

WAVERLEY

Fame is a fleeting thing, my friends. Today's headlines wrap up tomorrow's fish and chips, and after that they get shoved in a bin.

It's interesting to note, for example, that back when Melbourne was being built in the 1840s and 1850s, the most famous and successful novelist that the world had ever known was a man who is now hardly read. The first literary mega-star (take JK Rowling and multiply by ten), Sir Walter Scott essentially invented historical fiction with novels like *Waverley* and *Ivanhoe.*

Both titles, of course, lent their names to suburbs in Melbourne. As did Templestowe (a mythical place mentioned in *Ivanhoe*) and Abbottsford (the name of Scott's house).

WILLAURA

According to an old article in the *Sydney Morning Herald*, the Victorian town of Willaura owes its name to a 'little romance'.

It seems that in the district at the time there was considerable interest in the affairs of two young ladies, Laura and Helen, who were both being courted by the same young man. The question was 'Will Laura or Helen do it?' The surveyor was inspired to name the district Willaura and a nearby locality he called Helendoit.

WILSONS PROMONTORY

A place of pristine beaches and plump, green mountains, lush rainforests and rugged cliffs, Wilsons Promontory is not just the most southerly bit of mainland Australia, it could well be the most spectacular.

It seems only fitting, then, that this unique ecological wonderland should be named after some obscure guy who never went there. A friend of either George Bass or Matthew Flinders, Thomas Wilson was a merchant from London. And, basically, that's all we know.

Similar clouds of glory surround 'a man named Buller who worked in the British Colonial Office'. He happened to be a friend of the man who 'discovered' Mount Buller and, again, that's about all we know.

WINDSOR

Alcohol may occasionally tear families apart, but it also brings communities together.

For proof of this, you need look no further than Windsor, Springvale, Doncaster, Cheltenham and Craigieburn. All five Melbourne suburbs chose to adopt the name of their local pub.

YARCK

Being in the green Goulburn Valley, Yarck's not actually all that yuck. The name probably means something like 'river'.

YARRA RIVER

Sometimes good intentions are not enough. You also need a good translator.

Called 'Birrarrung' ('a place of mists and shadows') by the Wurundjeri people, Melbourne's main waterway became the 'Yarra' in 1835 thanks to a surveyor by the name of John Wedge who 'asked local aborigines what they called the cascading waters'.

Not understanding the question, they replied 'Yarro yarro'. Meaning 'it flows'.

YEA

Yay for Yea, it's a wonderful place, though the name is less upbeat than it seems. Originally 'Muddy Creek', the town changed its name to honour Colonel Lacy Yea, a soldier who was shot to bits in the course of the Crimean war.

Queensland

Queensland could have been called Saxon-Land. Or Cookland. Or Flindersland. Or British Columbia.

All were apparently options put to Queen Victoria when her signature created the new colony on 6 June 1859 (along with 'Clarence', after her mother's mansion, Clarence House). The official line was that she 'actually preferred the name British Columbia, but was won over when Colonial Secretary Sir Edward Bulwer-Lytton informed her that "the colonists would find particular pride" in Queen's Land'. According to the colony's first governor, however, the name was 'entirely the happy thought and inspiration of Her Majesty herself'.

A bit cheeky, really, given that it was not actually 'her' land at all. With around 200 nations and up to 500 000 people, Queensland was far and away the most populated place in Australia when the first white people arrived on its shores. And it remains far and away the most populated when it comes to

Indigenous place names, from Toowoomba and Toogoolawah to Thargomindah and Tinaroo.

On a less positive note, Indigenous people are also represented in place names like Massacre Island and Poisoned Waterhole Creek. Fighting between Aborigines and settlers was far more intense in colonial Queensland than anywhere else, and Indigenous casualties are thought to have exceeded 65000.

Everyday racism was fairly intense as well, of course, and to this day you can still find big, long 'Boundary streets' in Brisbane and Spring Hill, and 'Boundary roads' in Camp Hill, Bardon, Thornlands, Rocklea and Indooroopilly. They all signify the boundaries which nineteenth-century Indigenous people couldn't cross.

What about non-Indigenous names? Well, many of Queensland's – and, indeed, Australia's – came from a Dutchman called Willem Janszoon. Sailing south from Indonesia in 1606, he landed on the western shore of (what was later called) Cape York and named the 'Bush River' (or, rather: Rivier met het Bosch).

Rivier met het Bosch is now called the Pennefeather River – and that's certainly not the last Dutch name that we've ditched. The Gulf of Carpentaria and Cape Kerweer are two of only seven names which survive from their seventeenth-century voyages along Queensland's northern coast.

In 1770, it was Captain Cook's turn. Travelling from south to north, that navigator named no less than 86 places along Queensland's east coast. While his inspirations were generally geographical (North Head, Long Isle, Wide Sound and so forth), he wasn't shy when it came to honouring earls and dukes (Temple Bay, Moreton Bay, Hervey Bay, Dunk Island, Edgecumbe Bay, Cape Hillsborough, Cape York, Cape Bedford, Cape Gloucester, Cape Grafton), or assorted big shots back in the Admiralty (Cockburn Islands and capes Palmerston, Townshend and Cleveland).

Some of Captain Cook's other place names hint at the *Endeavour*'s trials and tribulations: Point Lookout, Point Danger, Hope Island, Weary Bay, plus of course Cape Tribulation. He 'discovered' the Whitsundays on Whitsunday, and took 'formal possession' at Possession Island.

The next explorer to venture there was Matthew Flinders, who named a few places after colleagues (Mount Larcom, Bentinck Island). Mount Archer, the Oxley River, and the towns of Leichhardt, Lansborough, Mitchell and Mackay all honour men who explored the interior of the state – but, of course, the best honours come with being a governor.

Originally called Edenglassie, a combination of Edinburgh and Glasgow, the town of Brisbane was founded when Sydneysiders petitioned New South Wales's Scottish-born governor, Thomas Brisbane, to find another place for the colony's worst convicts. Later New South Wales governors were also happy to see themselves on the map, which is why Queensland also has the Darling Downs, the Fitzroy River and Denison.

In 1859, Queensland became a stand-alone colony, thanks to Her Majesty the Queen. But it was all thanks to the first five stand-alone governors of Queensland that the state now has places like Blackhall, Bowen, Chermside, Cairns, Port Musgrave and Musgrave Hill.

But how on earth did it get places like Dicky Beach and Dead Mans Gully, let alone Wanka Creek and Wonglepong? Read on and I'll tell all.

ADAVALE

Do you have a veil?

Neither did Ada. Now home to about 15 people (and roughly 8 million mosquitoes and flies), Adavale is said to have been named after the wife of a surveyor, who lost her veil somewhere nearby.

ALBANY CREEK

Mount Nigger. Nigger Head. Niggers Bounce. At one time these were all Queensland place names, along with the charming Little Black Gin Creek.

There's still some work to be done, however, when it comes to wiping racism off the map. And it should start in Albany Creek. Once a major gold field with plenty of Chinese miners, this suburb in sunny Moreton Bay was originally called 'Chinamans Creek'. But then some white residents wrote to the government, requesting a change of name. 'Albany' sounded a little more appealing, they felt – not least because 'alb' comes from the Latin 'albus', meaning white.

ARAMAC

If I ever felt the urge to carve some words on a tree, I would probably carve 'Eamon Evans'. Robert Ramsay Mackenzie made a different choice, however (though this was largely because he had a different name).

Travelling north of Barcaldine in the 1850s, in search of a place to squat sheep, this 'physically large but intellectually limited' explorer carved the words 'RR Mac' on an old gum tree. The inscription was found years later by another explorer, William Landsborough, and was used to name the area. His spelling, however, was a little off. Maybe he was intellectually limited too?

ARANA HILLS

According to at least one local historian, the first residents of Arana Hills gave that name to their suburb because they were 'under the impression that in some Aboriginal languages it meant "welcome" ... The later discovery that it was a word referring to the moon did not take away from its pleasant-sounding ring'.

BANANA

Sail a ship off the coast of Queensland and you'll see Yam Island and Coconut Island. Sail inland and you'll eventually find Damper Creek. The state also boasts a Brandy Creek, a Butchers Creek and an Oyster Creek, together with a Nut Grove and a Mango Hill.

Queensland, this is to say, has plenty of places that are named after food.

But we should note that Banana is not one of them. That town's name apparently derives from a yellowish bullock who local stockmen used to herd cattle.

BARNEY POINT

Did you know there was once a colony called 'North Australia'?

No? Well, don't feel bad; it didn't last long. Basically North Australia was all of the Northern Territory plus the top half of Queensland, and was established by Britain's prime minister William Gladstone in 1846, with one George Barney appointed Lieutenant-Governor.

In January 1847, North Australia's newly appointed governor set sail from Sydney in order to start the first settlement. Probably the first sign that things were not going to go well was the fact that their ship ran aground, forcing Barney and the 88 settlers to camp at what's now Barney Point, in Gladstone.

The second sign was that camping sucked. 'It was mid-summer. It rained heavily. The temperature in the tents reached 110 degrees day after day. The colonists were tormented by mosquitoes. The Aborigines were hostile. Some of the settlers complained that Barney was dilatory and inde-cisive, and that for the first uncomfortable weeks nothing was done.'

But the real clincher, as far as bad signs went, was the fact that Gladstone then got voted out of office, and the new government lost no time in ditching his plans. In April 1847, the news finally reached Barney that Northern Australia was no more.

BONGAREE

Tracker, explorer, tribal elder. Fish salesman, snappy dresser, showman. It's safe to say that Bungaree was one of Sydney Cove's more colourful residents. A 'chief of the Broken Bay Tribe', his nicknames included 'King Bungaree', 'the king of Port Jackson' and 'the King of the Blacks'.

They did not, however, include Bongaree, which is a pity, as that suburb is named after him.

BOYLAND

This region got its name from George Boyland, a former chairman of Tamborine Shire Council. Not from whatever you were thinking.

BREAKFAST CREEK

Whether or not 'Brisbane' is a particularly good name, it's clearly better than 'Breakfast Creek'.

But Queensland's capital city could have been called just that, if John Oxley had had things his way. In 1823, that famous explorer 'discovered' the Brisbane River, naming it after Sir Thomas Brisbane, the governor of New South Wales. And it was along the banks of that river that the governor ordered a settlement to be built, which over time also adopted his name.

But Oxley's strong preference had been to build Queensland's first settlement at another one of his 'discoveries'. So named because he'd once breakfasted there, Breakfast Creek had 'good'

Brisbane

Anyone who's ever been to the Valley at 2 am might not be all that surprised to learn that the surname 'Brisbane' means 'to break bones'. The first 'Brisbane' was probably some sort of surgeon – but there's every chance that he was some kind of a torturer, or at least an amateur thug.

Anyway, the Brisbane that concerns us here was some sort of governor (though he was a soldier for a while before that). A major general under the Duke of Wellington who 'saw much action' during the Napoleonic Wars, Sir Thomas Brisbane was appointed Governor of New South Wales because Wellington owed him one and ... well ... that was about it, really. 'There are many brave men not fit to be governors of colonies,' the Duke admitted in 1825, when his protégé was recalled to England after just four years.

'A man of the best intentions, but disinclined to business, and deficient in energy,' Brisbane's biggest problem was controlling his subordinates, and it was a problem that he never quite solved. Falsely accused of using female convicts for 'immoral purposes', the 'amiable but weak' governor 'was rather out of his element when surrounded by the arrogance of the New South Wales magistracy, the disloyalty and factiousness of officials and the explosive rifts in colonial society'. His most bitter enemies included the Macarthurs and the Blaxlands (of federal electorate fame), John Oxley (now a town, school and suburb) and John Dunmore Lang (just think of Lang Park).

But it was Frederick Goulburn, of Goulburn Valley fame, who eventually proved his undoing. Brisbane's relationship with his colonial secretary was so poisonous and dysfunctional that the powers-that-be ordered both men home.

Before then, however, Brisbane did manage to send a few folk north and help them to start a new settlement. I think you can probably guess what they called it.

Albert Street *Prince Albert, Queen Victoria's husband*

Alice Street *Princess Alice, a daughter of Queen Victoria and the Grand Duchess of Hesse and by Rhine*

Bribie Island *From 'Bribie the basket maker', a former convict who frequently visited the island to get materials which he used for his baskets*

Charlotte Street *Princess Charlotte of Wales*

George Street *Prince George, Duke of Cambridge*

Kurilpa Bridge *'Place for water rats'*

Lang Park *John Dunmore Lang, early proponent of Australian independence*

Mary Street *Princess Mary, Duchess of Gloucester and Edinburgh*

Moreton Bay *James Douglas, 14th Earl of Morton (not 'Moreton')*

Queen Street *Queen Victoria*

Roma Street Parkland *Lady Diamantina Bowen (nee di Roma), wife of Sir George Bowen, Queensland governor, 1859–68*

Story Bridge *John Douglas Story, prominent public servant*

Tallebudgera Beach *'A good place to fish'*

Wickham Park *John Clements Wickham, first officer on board the HMS Beagle* soil and 'water in abundance', he argued, and was 'by no means an ineligible station for a first settlement up the river'.

BULCOCK BEACH

Named after Robert Bulcock, a Queensland MP. So no jokes please, you're better than that.

BUM BUM CREEK

Drive to Crows Nest along the New England Highway, and you might just see a sign saying 'Bum Bum Creek'. Chances are that you won't, however, as according to locals, 'it keeps getting nicked'.

BUSTARD BAY

Now, there's no doubt that Captain Cook knew how to navigate. He was a man you could trust to sail a sloop sou-sou-westerly while doing something or other with a jib-boom.

But we can't all be good at everything (as I say apologetically to my partner rather a lot). For all his easy familiarity with mizzenmasts, and constant readiness to use words like 'abaft', history shows us that once Captain Cook had 'discovered' a place, he wasn't so great at giving it a name.

Take Bustard Bay, for example. So named because it was there that his crew shot a 'bustard' (or scrub turkey), it's just one of many places in Queensland the short-on-ideas sailor named after an animal he saw. Tourists can also visit Lizard Island ('the only land Animals we saw here were lizards, and these seem'd to be pretty Plenty'), and Eagle Island (where he 'found a pretty number of birds').

Booby Island is also named after its population of birds (yes, I know, this came as a blow to me too), while Cape Dromedary, Pigeon House Mountain and Ram Head apparently look like a dromedary, a pigeon and a ram.

CANNIBAL CREEK

'A beautiful creek and a great spot to camp', Cannibal Creek in Cape York Peninsula has what you might call a memorable name.

Some people say it came about 'because it was here that a miner was allegedly killed and eaten by the indigenous inhabitants of the area'.

But, then again, some people will say anything. Best not to listen to them, really.

CANNON HILL

If a tree falls in the forest and no-one is around to hear it, does it make a sound? So goes a famous philosophical thought experiment, which touches on metaphysical theories like 'subjective idealism' and the 'anthropic principle' (whatever the hell they might be).

Rather less famous (and thankfully less philosophical) is the question of what a fallen tree *looks* like, after it lands on the ground. The answer is 'a bit like a cannon', according to the first settlers at what they called Cannon Hill.

CAPE TRIBULATION

How do you know when a planeload of English people has landed? The engine stops but the whining noise goes on. So goes a typical 'whinging Pom' joke, and if you don't like it, I have more.

By and large, of course, they are completely unfair. But in Captain Cook's case, possibly not. Cape Tribulation in Far North Queensland received its name in 1770, when the *Endeavour* scraped a reef and ran aground. 'I name this point Cape Tribulation,' he wrote, 'because here begun all my troubles.'

The next morning, it's said, 'he awoke in a particularly grumpy mood and proceeded to assign some very negative names to the places around him.'

CHERBOURG

With 35 wars between them so far, English people have had very little time for the French, and the French even less for the English. Personally, I think both views have their merits, but that's neither here nor there.

As a native of Cherbury, a charming village in Oxfordshire, it seems safe to assume that Richard Jones would have been a loyal Briton to his bootstraps, even after his move south to the colonies. We can at least be sure he felt some affection for Cherbury, as he gave the Queensland town which he founded that name.

And it seems even safer to assume he would regret the sloppy handwriting which resulted it being misread as 'Cherburg', and dutifully altered to 'Cherbourg' by a map maker.

Merde!

CLEVELAND

All we really know about the first Duke of Cleveland was that 'he seldom spoke in the House of Lords and that when he did his manner was better than his matter'.

But hey, he was a duke. And in 1840, that mattered a lot.

COOPERS PLAINS

Yet another example of good intentions being no match for bad spelling, this Brisbane suburb was named after Harry *Cow*per, one of Australia's earliest doctors.

D'AGUILAR

Army regulations in the early 1800s, according to Peter Burroughs, 'were more concerned with discipline and order, as the necessary basis of military efficiency and morale, than with the welfare and living conditions of the common soldier.'

This is what is known as an 'understatement'. You could be flogged for just about anything in the army, back then. For slouching. For shuffling. For being slow to salute. For failing to polish your boots so that they shone.

And you could be shot for almost everything else.

The man responsible for many of these rules was Sir George D'Aguilar, the author of *Regulations and Punishments of the British Army*, and, I'm guessing, a bit of a prat. He's also the man after whom the town of D'Aguilar is named, having been a friend of the then New South Wales governor.

DAYDREAM ISLAND

'It is a sad truth,' said Oscar Wilde, 'but we have lost the faculty of giving lovely names to things . . . The man who could call a spade a spade should be compelled to use one. It is the only thing he is fit for.'

Thankfully, things have changed since then, as a quick trip around Queensland shows. That state is full of places like Daydream Island . . . which, in Oscar's time, went by the name of 'West Molle Island'.

Point Cartwright, for its part, was originally known as Point Raper, while Chirnside was Downfall Creek. Kholo started out as Ugly Creek, and Stones Corner was Burnetts Swamp. Newmarket is no longer Three Mile Scrub and what's now Pinkenba was once Boggy Creek.

Even Abednego and Banoon received a spit and a polish. They're now Rose Hill and Sunnybank.

DEAD MANS GULLY

Truth is just a matter of perspective; right and wrong, just a state of mind.

From one point of view, for example, Dead Mans Gully in Far North Queensland would be a *bad* place for you or me to go swimming. But from a crocodile's perspective, nothing could be better. We should all strip off and go right now, in fact, and bring our family and friends.

DICKY BEACH

Named after a stranded ship, the SS *Dicky*, which was named after God-knows-what.

DUYFKEN POINT

A lush, green headland in the Gulf of Carpentaria, Duyfken Point was probably the first part of Australia to be seen by European eyes.

Those eyes belonged to the captain of a Dutch trading ship, the *Duyfken*, which sailed south from Indonesia to see what was there some 164 years before Captain Cook.

Captain Willem Janszoon charted 320 kilometres of coastline with tremendous skill – but a tremendous explorer he possibly wasn't. Until his dying day, he believed that he'd actually been charting a southerly stretch of *New Guinea*. And that Western Australia, which he visited a few years later, was in fact just a biggish island.

ERMARA

'Where it is always raining.'

FORTITUDE VALLEY

Unless you happen to enjoy watching drunken teenagers fight, spew and – worst of all – talk, a night out in Brisbane's Fortitude Valley definitely requires a great deal of fortitude.

But that's not how it picked up the name. Like Mermaid Waters on the Gold Coast and Amity Point in North Stradbroke, the area is named after the ship that brought its first settlers on the long journey from north to south.

Coolangatta, for its part, is also named after a boat. But the *Coolangatta* was just a cargo ship – or, at least, it was until it happened to get wrecked there.

FRASER ISLAND

Being a great sandy island, Fraser Island was once called Great Sandy Island, Captain Cook having chosen the name with his customary dash and flair.

And Great Sandy Island it would have remained were it not for Eliza Fraser. The wife of the captain of the *Stirling Castle*, she would later become his widow. In 1836 the ship scraped a reef and sank near what's now Rockhampton. What happened next is open to conjecture, but it seems the captain, Eliza and some of her crewmates somehow survived and swam to Great Sandy Island, where they were either captured or adopted by a local tribe.

According to the *Australian Dictionary of Biography*, the tribal women 'cleansed Eliza's sunburned body with sand, rubbed it with charcoal and decorated it with colour and feathers. She was required to nurse their children, dig fern roots and rob bees nests, but was so inept and resentful that the women tormented her. She witnessed the death of her husband, after he was speared. His first mate also died and two seamen drowned attempting to swim the strait. Fed on scraps and taken by canoe to the mainland, but not permitted to contact the other castaways, Eliza felt herself a slave.'

But *was* she? All we know for certain is that, after somebody 'rescued' her, she lost little time soliciting 'a large sum of money' through a public appeal. 'A most profane, artful and wicked woman,' according to at least one acquaintance, Eliza then remarried and took a boat back to England, where she launched a second public appeal for funds, describing herself as 'a penniless widow'.

GHOST HILL

As ghost stories go, I'm sorry to say that this one is fairly dull. Not quite as dull, perhaps, as *A Nightmare on Elm Street 5*, but every bit as scary – in the sense that it's not scary at all.

Anyway, here goes. Back in the early days of Hervey Bay, Ghost Hill was just called 'the Hill'. But all that changed one windy night when one of its residents was late coming home. His wife grabbed a lamp and went out to look for him, wearing a large white nightie which flapped in the wind. From the bottom of the hill, it was thought she looked like a ghost, and so a new name for her suburb was born.

GLADSTONE

Four times prime minister of Great Britain, and a four-time Chancellor of the Exchequer as well, William Gladstone was one of those Great Men of History: he was a colossus who strode the world stage. When you consider his efforts to expand the vote, and reform relations with Ireland, it's no surprise that the town of Gladstone was named after him – especially given that he was in office around the time it was settled.

What *is* surprising, perhaps, are his hobbies. Along with chopping down trees for fun – he liked to fell an oak every couple of days – the evangelical statesman apparently spent his spare time wandering London's dark, lonely streets looking for prostitutes whom he felt he could 'save'.

GOAT ISLAND

Once considered a good place to run goats, due to its absence of foxes, this island is *not*, in fact, a good place to run goats. No sir, not a good place at all. Several farmers discovered this in 1916, when the river flooded and drowned all their herds.

GOLD COAST

Could Captain Cook see into the future? It's certainly tempting to think so, for when he sailed along Queensland's southern coast, he gave places on it names like Point Danger and Mount Warning.

Those places, of course, now form a part of the Gold Coast: Australia's answer to some vulgar question that really should not have been asked. Filled with bogans, bikies, schoolies and strippers, this 50-kilometre strip of sun, sand and surf was originally called the South Coast, it being south of Brisbane.

The 1950s, however, brought a real estate boom. Land prices doubled, and then doubled again. 'It was reported over the radio in about 1957 that the boom was literally like making "gold on the coast" . . . and a reporter who has not been identified [then] coined a simple phrase.'

GOODNA

Goodna's name may not be so good, if urban legend is to be believed. The story goes that when settlers arrived in the area and ordered its original inhabitants to make themselves scarce, they also asked a local elder what exactly the land was called.

'Goodna', he supposedly answered. A word which, according to legend, actually just means 'shit'.

GUNPOWDER

We don't know what might have happened to give this mining town its unusual name. But, if you were an Aborigine who lived somewhere nearby, I suspect it wasn't good.

HELLS GATE

Whoever said that crime doesn't pay had clearly never been to the gold fields. There was no need to buy a spade to get your hands on a nugget. A gun, a horse and a good place to hide would do the job just as well.

Hells Gate was apparently one such place. A bush track between Cooktown and the Palmer River gold fields, it was full of miners carrying bags full of gold, and bushrangers lying in wait.

The fact that the bumpy 170-mile (about 275-kilometre) track could also feature crocodiles, snakes and hostile Aborigines, together with a hot sun and not much water, meant that, as one traveller put it, 'it was like passing through the gates of hell'.

HERSTON

Back in the nineteenth century, homosexuality was the love that dared not speak its name.

It could, however, name a suburb. 'Herston' in inner-city Brisbane got its name from a farmhouse shared by two bachelors. Room mates at Oxford, Sir Robert *Her*bert, Queensland's first premier, and Sir Robert Bram*ston*, his devoted friend, moved to Australia together and were rarely apart.

HERVEY BAY

Augustus Hervey, the man after whom Captain Cook named Hervey Bay, was a British admiral and politician who eventually became Earl of Bristol.

But, really, who cares about that? The son of a blue-blooded cross-dresser, Hervey's main claim to fame was a bigamy trial – together with 'a libidinous appetite which would have shamed a rampant stag'. Several nuns were numbered among the English Casanova's hundreds of conquests, along with well-known opera singers and married aristocrats, and the mistress of Frederick the Great.

HUMPYBONG

These days we tend to think that whenever a settler went and got settled somewhere, it was only a matter of time before others followed suit.

In fact, it was a far more haphazard process, some settlements having been, well, crap.

Humpybong, for example, could have been bigger than Brisbane – but it's now just an obscure little place to its north. The very first place to be settled in Queensland, Humpybong rapidly became the first place to be abandoned, thanks to poor anchorage and endless mosquitoes. Its residents left behind lots of empty shelters, which local Aborigines labelled 'oompie bong' – a phrase meaning 'dead houses'.

HUNCHY

Ciggie. Mozzie. Journo. Dero. Australians love to shorten words and, every so often, that's not a bad thing. The Sunshine Coast suburb of Hunchy, for example, used to go by the name of 'Hunchback'.

INDOOROOPILLY

'Gully of the leeches.'

KIELS MOUNTAIN

If I wanted to be pedantic (which, of course, I often do), I would point out that the Sunshine Coast suburb of Kiels Mountain was actually named after a settler called Henry *Keil*.

Did you notice how the 'i' in his name actually comes *after* the 'e'? Well, neither did later map makers.

Carseldine, a few kilometres away, had similar problems. It was settled by a builder named William Castle*dean*.

KUREELPA

'Place of rats.'

LAMINGTON NATIONAL PARK

A former governor of Queensland, the 2nd Baron Lamington, is best known for the choc-covered sponge cake that someone invented in his honour at some function.

But to my mind he should be remembered for his commitment to conservation – or what you might call a lack thereof. In 1899, Lord Lamington was invited by local conservationists to inspect a forest which they felt ought to be turned into a national park. He went along, and in due course agreed, but it's worth noting he also brought a gun . . . and used it to shoot a koala.

LOGAN CREEK

If you were applying for a job as a convict overseer, you would have had no need to call yourself a team player with solid project management skills and proficiency in Microsoft Word. You didn't need initiative or the ability to self-motivate. All you needed to be was a bit of a prick.

Captain Patrick Logan was a major prick. In charge of around 1000 convicts in Moreton Bay, he felt his job was to make them as miserable as possible, and it was a job that he did very well. Fond of making them move big rocks from dawn until dark, 'the Fell Tyrant' would only ever allow time off so his charges could watch someone get whipped.

Logan himself, however, *did* deserve a break, so every now and then he took one. They generally took the form of exploring the region – until, on one such expedition, he was killed by an Indigenous man.

Or was he? The next day, it is said, some convicts were working on what's now Logan Creek when they saw their captain alive and well on the other side of the riverbank. 'None had any doubts about who it was.' Not knowing that he was supposed to be dead, two of them downed tools, hastily launched the punt used to ferry people across the river and rowed over to pick him up. '[But] when they arrived on the south bank . . . there was no sign of Logan. He and his horse had vanished into thin air . . . At that time Captain Logan's battered body was growing cold in a shallow grave in the bush seventy kilometres inland.'

MAGNETIC ISLAND

If at first you don't succeed, blame the magnetic properties of a nearby island.

When Captain Cook sailed past what's now Townsville, his compass did not 'travis well'. The problem, he reasoned, was mostly likely a large deposit of iron ore on that island nearby, since it clearly boasted 'the most rugged, rocky and barrenest Surface of any we have yet seen'.

It was a perfectly good theory, apart from the fact that it was completely wrong. Magnetic Island contains no large iron deposit, and isn't magnetic at all.

MARYLAND

Located about 100 kilometres south of Toowoomba, and right next to nothing at all, Maryland is a rural idyll – that is, a place where there's nothing to do.

It's said that once upon a time, however, three young settlers found a way to fill in some time. Fearing an attack from the local Aborigines, it seems that 'Matthew Marsh, Charles Marsh and Charles Perrot imbibed too heavily in rum to bolster their courage'.

The attack didn't happen, but a great party *did*, so they began calling the area *Merry*lands – a great name that was eventually tweaked.

MISSION BEACH

A 'mission' is, in theory at least, an effort to in some way do good. Some missions seek justice, others provide health care, and a bunch of them just bang on about God.

The Hull River Aboriginal Mission, on the other hand, was essentially one big jail. An initiative of the Queensland government, it was an attempt to keep Aboriginal people a long way away from white settlers – even if they had to be taken in chains.

MOFFAT HEAD

We don't know much about James C Moffat, a Brisbane chemist with a Sunshine Coast holiday house, but I think it's safe to say he wasn't easily embarrassed.

In 1883, you see, this Moffat formed a syndicate with his Sunshine Coast neighbours in order to buy a big strip of land. After selling a big chunk of it, he suggested that the syndicate subdivide the rest, and organised a raffle to see who got which bit.

Moffat Head was far and away the most attractive and valuable piece of land. And I think that we can all guess who won it.

MOUNT BOTTLE AND GLASS

My advice to anyone who's thinking about mountain-climbing would be to think about something else.

If they're really determined to do it, however, and somehow manage to escape their asylum, my other advice would be: bring lots of water. Thirst may well be the worst thing about hiking (though it's hard to know for sure: there are so many candidates).

Wine, on the other hand, is a less useful item, which may be why someone left behind a bottle and glass halfway up what's known as Mount Bottle And Glass.

MOUNT BREAST

I think you should be able to work this one out.

MOUNT COOLUM

With its thick green grass and spectacular sheer cliffs, Mount Coolum actually looks rather nice. But for God's sake, don't be fooled, good people: it's actually a headless corpse.

According to an ancient Dreamtime legend, Coolum was a nice young man who was once engaged to Maroochy, a beautiful girl. But the happy couple ceased to be happy – or, for that matter, a couple – when Ninderry, a warrior from a rival tribe, kidnapped Maroochy in order to marry her himself.

Coolum naturally went off in pursuit of Ninderry, but when he found him, things didn't go well. Ninderry threw a club at his head, which rolled into the sea and became Mudjimba Island. Coolum's headless body, meanwhile, turned into stone and became what we now call Mount Coolum.

Maroochy, distraught, wept so much that her tears can be seen to this day flowing down the Maroochy River.

There is, however, at least some justice in the world. For it seems that 'the Spirit God had been watching these events from his crystal throne in the sky and was deeply incensed by Ninderry's foul deed'. He 'struck down Ninderry and turned him into stone' – or, rather, a summit called 'Ninderry Crest'.

MOUNT COOT-THA

Once upon a time, this fairly bare Brisbane mountain was known as 'One Tree Hill'.

Sensing that it might be a good idea to come up with a name that wasn't crap, a parliamentary clerk went to an Indigenous elder in 1880 to ask him what name his people used. 'King

Sandy' gave him two options – and the clerk sadly chose the one that means 'place of honey'.

The fun alternative, it much later emerged, was 'Mappee', a word meaning 'bum'.

MOUNT MEE

Some puns are just so obvious – so thuddingly crude and lewd – that the sophisticated prose stylist will refrain from pointing them out.

Not being a sophisticated prose stylist, I'm happy to say that Mount Mee is a name that merits a bit of a smirk. Less entertaining, however, is the explanation behind it. 'Mee' comes from 'mia-mia', a word in the local Indigenous language that simply means 'view' or 'lookout'.

MOUNT UPSTART

No, there's nothing at all arrogant about this Far North Queensland mountain. As far as I know, it keeps itself to itself, and has never said anything vulgar or brash.

So why is it such an upstart? Well, the name just comes from the way it's 'surrounded with low land' but then 'starts and rises up singley at the first making of it,' as Captain Cook not-very-clearly explains.

MUCKADILLA

If you ever drove to Muckadilla, a hot, dry town in the hot, dry outback, you would not think that it had 'plenty of water'. But this is in fact what its ancient name means.

In 1880, settlers realised why. There's plenty of water under the ground. With an expensive and state-of-the-art water bore, they transformed the town 'into a fancy health resort as it was thought the sulphur-rich artesian water could heal a range of ailments such as rheumatism and arthritis'.

We now know that it can't, however, and the 'famous Muckadilla Baths' are no more. The town still has plenty of water, but visitors are in short supply.

PIMPIMBUDGEE

Apologies, but I haven't been able to discover how this stretch of bush got its name. But leaving it out just wasn't an option.

POEPPEL CORNER

If you drive for hours and hours through the Simpson Desert, and then continue for a couple more weeks, you will eventually come across something that isn't just road, sand or scrub.

Don't get too excited, however (presuming that you can still remember what excitement might feel like). It's only a great, big plaque. It represents the exact spot where the state of Queensland meets the state of South Australia, not to mention the Northern Territory as well.

It's called Poeppel Corner after Augustus Poeppel, a surveyor who spent 20 months battling flies, heat and dust in order to lay out the length of each state with a chain. Identifying the precise spot where all three met was painstaking and profoundly complicated work.

And that may explain why he mucked it up. The plaque was moved to its present spot a few years ago. The original 'Poeppel Corner' was 330 yards (about 300 metres) east.

PRIESTS GULLY

This little gully in the outer suburbs of Brisbane represents the spot where a priest once got lost.

Unfortunately, he was later found.

PROSERPINE

With its rich black soil, tropical rains and warm sun, the town of Proserpine is wonderfully fertile, which is presumably why a settler named it after the ancient Greek Goddess of Fertility.

But we're entitled to feel some doubt about his choice. Proserpine did, after all, marry her uncle. Her uncle was Hades, ruler of the underworld: a pain-filled, dark and fiery chamber filled with the lost souls of the dead.

RESTORATION ISLAND

If we were to create some sort of ranking system for history's most successful leaders, Captain William Bligh would end up somewhere between Billy McMahon and an ingrown toenail that's turning green.

Blessed with a 'gift, that almost amounted to genius, for insulting and infuriating his immediate subordinates', Bligh is said to have been 'an overbearing control freak' who was 'pedantic about protocol', 'obsessed with detail' and 'quick to humiliate anyone who failed to meet his perfectionist standards'.

It was not a great way to win friends on the *Bounty*, a small cargo ship which set sail from Tahiti in order to take breadfruit plants to the West Indies. But it was a great way to inspire a mutiny. Bligh was hauled out of his bed by a crew armed with cutlasses, and cast adrift on a raft.

Over the next 47 days, he and a handful of loyal officers drifted for 3618 nautical miles (6700 kilometres). And he managed to annoy them every step of the way. Their first stop was an island off Far North Queensland. Blight named it Restoration Island because the food they found there helped to restore their strength, and thus allowed him to see off yet another mutiny, by challenging an 'insubordinate' officer to a duel.

That certainly wasn't Bligh's last experience of 'insubordination', however. He was thrown off another boat, the *Nore*, a decade or so later.

And nor was it his last time in Australia. In 1805, he was appointed governor of New South Wales. And promptly inspired a military coup.

ROBA

'Plenty of goannas.'

ST HELENA ISLAND

Napoleon was not what you'd call a hands-on soldier. He liked to spend battles well away from the bullets, in a tent with cushions and food.

The result was that the French emperor did not die at Waterloo (though he did, apparently, complain a great deal of haemorrhoids). He was, rather, captured after that final battle with the British, and sent to spend his final days on St Helena Island, a remote spot in the Atlantic Ocean, with British soldiers on all sides.

That was all in 1815. And 12 years later, it happened again. But the exile *this* time was not a short, fat Frenchman whose favourite hobby was 'conquering Europe'. It was a short, fat

Aboriginal man who received the nickname 'Napoleon' as he apparently looked kind of similar.

This Napoleon got in the bad books with some settlers one day when he was caught stealing their axe. 'By way of punishment, they took him over to this island in the bay and left him there – jokingly naming it St Helena.'

Unlike his namesake, however, he managed to escape. Napoleon made a bark canoe and paddled back the next day.

TANNUM SANDS

Skin cancer wasn't really something to worry about, way back in the 1930s. Originally known as Wild Cattle Creek, the town of Tannum Sands supposedly received its current name when a Lands Department official saw a group of kids return from a Sunday School picnic with bright red, sunburnt skin. 'We can really tan 'em over here,' one of the supervisors boasted, and the official thought, *What a good name.*

TINAROO

Have you ever heard anyone say 'harroo'? No, me neither. As a word, it's a bit like 'tally-ho' or 'pip pip' . . . that is, not actually a word.

But say 'harroo' someone apparently did, when he discovered alluvial tin in the Atherton Tablelands. 'Tin harroo!' shouted John Atherton, thus giving the town of Tinaroo its name.

TIN CAN BAY

The good news is that there are no tin cans in Tin Can Bay. The name probably comes from the word 'tuncanbar', a word meaning 'dugongs'.

The bad news, however, is that there really is a doctor in Doctors Creek. 'Doctor' was the name of a horse who got stuck on its banks, and unfortunately stayed stuck until he drowned.

TINGALPA

There are many different theories as to what Tingalpa means. But my favourite is 'fat kangaroo'.

TOOWOOMBA

There's no such thing as a 'Toowoomba' in any Indigenous language, but there are a few words that come pretty close. A 'tawampa', for example, is a local word for swamp, while 'woomba woomba' means 'lots of reeds'.

Residents of the southern Queensland town can also chomp on 'choowooms', if they choose: it's the name of a local melon.

TOWNSVILLE

So Townsville, are you a town or a village? It's probably time you made up your mind.

Actually, this tropical metropolis is a city. But it's a city that was founded by a cotton grower, a man named Robert Towns.

WANKA CREEK

We can only speculate why this Bulloo Downs waterway ended up with this name. But maybe it's best that we don't.

WEBYA DOWNS

'Place of stingrays.'

WHO'DA THOUGHT IT HILL

Who thought of this name and, above all, why? The answer is sadly unclear.

WITTA

'Wild dogs' or 'dingos'. This seems as good an opportunity as any to mention that the world's longest structure is not the Great Wall of China (which is actually more than one wall). It's Australia's very own Dingo Fence: 5614 kilometres of high wire mesh that stretches from the Sunshine Coast to the Great Australian Bight.

Designed to keep dingos and the like out of Australia's (comparatively) fertile south-east, the fence is actually north-west of Witta, so that town may now need a new name.

WONGLEPONG

No-one quite knows what Wonglepong means, but at the end of the day, who cares?

WOOLLOONGABBA

'Get ready for a f#@$ing broken arm,' Australian cricketer Michael Clarke once said during a fraught moment at the Gabba. It was not, all things considered, one of cricket's great moments of sportsmanship – but when it comes to fighting talk, the Gabba's seen worse.

Woolloongabba, the south Brisbane suburb where the stadium is based, is thought to mean something like 'place for fight talk'. It was where warring Aboriginal tribes could meet to discuss the rules of warfare, before getting on with the war itself.

YORKEYS KNOB

A knob, as we know, is a hill-like protuberance, and Lord knows there's nothing funny about that. But this Yorkey fellow deserves a mention as well.

According to one source, he was some sort of entrepreneur who insisted that sea cucumbers were a great aphrodisiac.

But whatever his skills as a salesman, Yorkey was a little less capable when it came to fishing. And, unfortunately, he liked to use dynamite instead of a net. One fishing trip saw him blow off his arm, and 'how he sailed his little sloop overnight to Cairns without complete blood loss remains a mystery to this day'.

Tasmania

In seventeenth-century Europe, spices were the spice of life. The wealthy were prepared to pay almost anything for nutmeg, cloves, mace and the like – exotic Asian wonder fruits which could make rotten meat less revolting, and bland food not bad.

The only problem was that they were, well, Asian – but that was a problem the Dutch traders felt able to solve. In the early 1600s, they set up a port in what's now Indonesia, and started to dabble in the spice – and slave – trades.

But they never forgot that the fabled Terra Australis must be somewhere to the south of them – and who knew what spices grew there? In 1642, then, the Dutch port's governor, Anthony Van Diemen, sent one of his merchants south-east, to see what there was to see. Sailing all the way south-west to Madagascar, and from there directly east, he sighted a brand new landmass on 29 November, and named it Van Diemen's Land after his boss.

But while Abel Tasman may have been the first foreigner to set his eyes on the place in about 14 000 years, he apparently didn't bother to set foot on it. He just sailed on through what's now the Tasman Sea, with the result that he 'discovered' New Zealand as well. (If you've ever wondered, that country gets its name from Zeeland – that is, 'Sea Land' – a bunch of boggy islands in the Netherlands, two of which it vaguely resembles.)

What he hadn't discovered, however, was any kind of viable trading post. Tasman was ticked off by Van Diemen, upon his return, for wasting the port's money and time. And that was thus it, when it came to Dutch contact with Tasmania, though remnants of it can still be found in about a dozen other place names. Frederick Hendrick Bay, De Witt Island and the like were all named by Abel after friends and acquaintances.

The next 130 years were like the 14 000 before: Van Diemen's Land had no visitors at all. Then, between 1772 and 1802, there came a big bunch of French boats, and quite a few English ones too. Ostensibly there out of 'scientific interest', the French expeditions by the likes of Louis de Freycinet, Marion du Fresne, Huon De Kermadec and Bruni d'Entrecasteaux left their marks in places like Freycinet, Marion Bay, the Huon Valley, Bruny Island and the D'Entrecasteaux Channel.

A 1799 English expedition by Matthew Flinders and George Bass, meanwhile, confirmed that Van Diemen's Land was definitely an island (one that is still separated from the mainland by the Bass Strait). What this discovery meant, in strictly legal terms, was that the English claim to the east coast of New Holland did not actually include Van Diemen's Land.

That island was technically Napoleon's for the taking if the English didn't get there first.

In 1802, therefore, they got there first. That new settlement – Australia's second-oldest – was named after Lord Robert Hobart, the Secretary of State for War and the Colonies, and the shout-outs to foreign dignitaries didn't stop there. Tasmania has three places named after Lord Hobart's colleagues (Hamilton, Bicheno and Sullivans Bay), while Derby, Rosebery, Stanley and Beaconsfield were all named after British prime ministers. George Town and Queenstown got their names from a king and a queen; Dunalley from a prominent baron; Mount Wellington, Clarence and Cape Portland from three different dukes.

But the governors of Van Diemen's Land were also keen to recognise *local* dignitaries . . . specifically, the governors of Van Diemen's Land. Collinsvale, Port Davey, Mount Sorell, Port Arthur, Wilmot and the Franklin River were all named after the first men in charge of the new colony . . . by the first men in charge of the new colony.

But the governors of New South Wales were technically in charge of *them*, which meant that they occasionally got a gig too. Latrobe, Macquarie Heads, Macquarie Pass and King Island all commemorate the time when Van Diemen's Land was a sort of junior colony – as does Launceston, which was named after a New South Wales governor's home town.

That's not the only British place name on the map, of course: there are dozens (for example, Devonport). Indigenous place names are pretty thin on the ground, however, because so too were Indigenous people. It's estimated that there were only around 5000 of them living on the island when the Brits first came to 'settle' it – and there can be no doubt that that number then shrank. Thanks to warfare, dispossession and infectious disease, there were almost no native Tasmanians left by the 1860s, and explorers, map makers and surveyors had almost no interest in picking their brains.

There were no convicts left by then, either: the colony became wholly self-governing on 1 January 1856, and closed the door on its penal past. It officially became 'Tasmania' on that date as well – the feeling being that Van Diemen's Land was just too closely associated with the convict past. Their memory lives on in places like the Gates of Hell and the Isle of the Dead, however – and from then on things get even more weird. Tasmania is home to some frankly odd place names. Sit back, and let these ones sink in.

ADVENTURE BAY

I would happily buy a book called *Adventure Bay* – in fact, one day I might just write one.

But it would need to be a work of fiction. The story of the *real* Adventure Bay, on the east coast of Tasmania's Bruny Island, does not actually involve any derring-do. There are no daring escapes, or dashing young swordsmen, or dewy-eyed maidens trapped in villainous lairs. It just happened to be the place where a cargo ship called the HMS *Adventure* docked for a couple of days.

BADGER HEAD

As the father of one of the world's girliest girls – a five-year-old who will only ever wear pink, and uses a texta to paint her nails – I long for the day when she loses all interest in fairies and starts playing pirates instead.

Maybe I should take her to Badger Head? It is, after all, named after a fine female role model: a woman who was sent to the colonies in chains, but somehow managed to seize control of the ship.

> Charlotte Badger's involvement (in the mutiny) varies from version to version. In some, she's dressed like a man, waving around a pistol, inciting everyone to riot. In others she's just swept up in the machinations of the other prisoners. In some she's credited with flogging members of the crew in return for how she was treated. Who knows?

Whatever the real story (and they all basically end there), Charlotte Badger is regarded as Australia's first female pirate. And if my daughter's generation is any guide to the future, she is probably also our last.

BASS STRAIT

Was George Bass straight?

Well, if a recently unearthed letter from his friend and shipmate, Matthew Flinders, is any guide, I'm guessing that the answer is no. 'There was a time, when I was so completely wrapped up in you, that no conversation but yours could give me any degree of pleasure,' Flinders wrote to the man who kept him company aboard the *Norfolk*, during all those long, lonely nights at sea. 'Your footsteps on the quarterdeck over my head, took me from my book, and brought me upon deck to walk with you . . .'

But while he named the Bass Strait after George, we should note that Flinders also named South Australia's Cape Wiles. 'And yet it is not clear to me that I love you entirely,' his letter continued. 'My affection for [the *Norfolk*'s botanist, Andrew] Wiles reaches farther into my heart. I would take him into the same skin as me!'

Ménage à trois? Je ne sais pas.

BATTERY POINT

Did you know that Russia and France once planned to invade Tasmania?

No? Well, I'm not sure if they did either. But the British Empire's *fear* of such an invasion was, at least, very real, and to assuage it they built lots of defences. Included among them was a battery of guns in central Hobart, in the suburb now known as Battery Point.

BAY OF FIRES

Such a great name deserves a great story. According to Tasmania's Parks & Wildlife Service, it 'was given to the area by Captain Tobias Furneaux, in 1773, when he noticed numerous fires along the coast. This led him to believe that the country was densely populated. Abundant evidence of this occupation by Aboriginal people can be seen along the coast today.'

Sorry, not a great story. Life can be like that sometimes.

BEAUTY POINT

Tasmania, as has often been noted, is not exactly a metropolitan hub. While other states like to boast about their nightlife – their busy cafes and crowded restaurants, their colourful bars and pulsating clubs – Tasmanians tend to go to bed early, so they're ready to spend the next day doing not much.

But, on the upside, the state's very beautiful. And if you don't believe me, take a look at the map. Among Tassie's untouched forests and crystal-clear lakes you'll find places with names like Paradise, Promised Land, Snug and Nook, not to mention the Golden Valley.

There's also a spot called 'Beauty Point', but I wouldn't necessarily suggest you spend all your time there. It was named after a lost cow called Beauty, as it was there that she was finally found.

BICHENO

The British Colonial Secretary for Van Diemen's Land from 1843–51, James Ebenezer Bicheno, had a long and distinguished career that was chock-full with all sorts of achievements. But all that needs to concern us here is that he was so very fat he could apparently fit three full bags of wheat into his trousers.

BLACK CHARLIES OPENING

No comment.

BLACKMANS BAY

Don't go leaping to conclusions, for you may just fall on your face. I'm pleased to report that the place name Blackmans Bay does not actually have racial overtones at all. It's a nod to James Blackman, an early white settler, not some Indigenous guy whose name wasn't important because his identity was defined by his skin colour.

No, sir. That would be Tasmania's *other* Blackmans Bay, the one near Dunalley.

BOOBYALLA

I was hoping to write something fairly racy here, but have found the material a bit hard to work with.

Nowadays more or less a ghost town, the Tassie port of Boobyalla got its name from some kind of plant. The scientific names of the two candidates are *Acacia longifolia* or 'any of several Australian trees of the genus *Myoporum*', and if you can make a sexual pun out of either of them, then please write in and let me know.

COLLINSVALE

Whatever you might think about its gun laws, health system and immigration policies (little hint: they're all pretty bad), there's no doubt that the US of A has done pretty well with its Founding Fathers. Jefferson. Washington. Franklin. Adams. They weren't just men of reason, they were all men of action as well. They fought the good fight for life and liberty. You might even describe them as warrior-poets.

Australia, on the other hand, tends to battle somewhat when it comes to our nation's first statesmen.

Take David Collins, for example: the first Lieutenant-Governor of New South Wales, and the man from whom Collinsvale and about three million Collins streets all get their rather dull name. As far as I can tell, he didn't do much. Other than once order a judicial inquiry into the loss of a cabbage.

DISMAL SWAMP

If you don't have anything nice to say, then you might enjoy making maps in Tasmania. Together with Little Hell, Mouldy Hole and Stinking Creek, that state also offers the lush allure of Cape Barren, together with that tourist magnet, Misery Bluff.

Whether or not the worst convicts were sent to Van Diemen's Land, it definitely got the whiniest.

DOO TOWN

You know the phrase 'an oldie but a goodie'? Well, some jokes are both old and *bad*.

A small collection of holiday houses a bit south of Hobart, Doo Town was named in the 1930s after a whimsical resident called his cottage 'Doo I'. Two of his neighbours then got in on the act, naming their houses 'Doo-Me' and 'Doo-Us'. Much guffawing quickly ensued, along with some slapping of thighs. Good times.

If you're thinking about going to Doo Town today, however, my advice is Doo Not. Literally every cottage is owned by a comedian, with names ranging from Da Doo Ron Ron,

Didgeri-Doo and Doo-All, to Doo Come In, Doodle Doo, Doo Drop In, Doo For Now, Doo Fuck All, Doo-ing It Easy, Doo Little, Doo Luv It, Doo Nix, Doo Nothing, Doo Often, Doo Us Too, Doo Write, Gunnadoo, Humpty Doo, Just Doo It, Love Me Doo, Make Doo, Much-A-Doo, Rum Doo, Sheil Doo, This Will Doo, Thistle Doo Me, Wattle-I-Doo, Wee-Doo, Xanadoo and a Yabba Dabba Doo.

Well, *almost* every cottage. You'll also see a house named 'Medhurst'. Now that *is* funny.

THE EDGE OF THE WORLD

If you're scared of edges, it might be a good idea to avoid Arthur River. (Though this advice probably holds even if you *aren't* scared of edges, as there are no hotels or restaurants or pubs.)

Anyway, 'acrophobics' (thank you, Wikipedia) are especially well-advised to avoid this spot, where the Arthur River meets the sea. Sure, it's just a remote and windy beach. But it's also a remote and windy beach with a plaque that says 'The Edge of the World'.

EGGS AND BACON BAY

Eating bacon, the World Health Organization recently informed us, is basically a slow form of suicide. The cured meat doesn't just lead to heart disease and diabetes, it can cause cancer in all sorts of places.

The dilemma, of course, is that it also tastes great. But I'm pleased to report that this is a dilemma Lady Jane Franklin was spared. The wife of an early Tassie governor (Sir John, of Franklin River fame), her ladyship lived long before pesky researchers started trying to help us to live longer, and she liked to eat her breakfast with a good view of a bay. So often did she have eggs and bacon at what was then called South Deep Bay, it soon joined Bream Creek, Oyster Cove, Punchbowl and Wineglass Bay as Tassie places named after food.

ELECTRONA

Did you know that much of Tasmania's electricity comes from Electrona?

Well, if so, you've been misinformed.

Now home to a couple of houses and factories – and, all in all, that's about it – this southern Tassie town used to house a huge hydroelectric power station, which slowly became less huge. And then smallish. And then shut.

HAUNTED BAY

No ghosts here, sadly. Just fairy penguins who make spooky noises.

THE HAZARDS

The Hazards are not that hazardous. A bunch of granite mountains named after a whaler called Richard Hazard, they can be climbed in safety by anyone who so wishes, and safely ignored by everyone else.

Don't go getting too comfortable, however. Danger may still be lurking in Tasmania's Break-Me-Neck Hill, and don't expect good times on Miserable Island. Hard Struggle Gully sounds a bit challenging, and do be careful if you go near Cape Grim.

HELLS GATES

'Abandon hope, all ye who enter here' advises the sign above the Gates of Hell in a famous passage from Dante's *Inferno*.

But the mere fact that something is in writing doesn't mean that it's actually right. Just look at the Bible. Or any tabloid newspaper.

Anyway, if you visit Hells Gates down in Tasmania, you won't find any doom-laden signs – or, indeed, any actual gates. You'll see exactly the same thing the people who named it saw: the mouth of Macquarie Harbour. Only, you being you, and the time being now, you'll then go back to your hotel, and pour some wine.

The convicts, however, had no such option. 'The most remote penal hellhole in the British Empire', Macquarie Harbour really was the entrance to hell.

ISLE OF THE DEAD

Not all convicts found Port Arthur a living hell, though this was only because some of them died. Their corpses were buried on a nearby island, which was given an appropriately cheerful name.

JERICHO

My knowledge of the Old Testament perhaps isn't all that it could be. I *do* know that God feels very strongly about wearing 'clothing made of two different types of material' (big no-no, don't do it) and can dimly recall scenes of rape, murder and incest (none of which He seems to much mind).

Hugh Germain, however, really knew his stuff. A British-born soldier and explorer, he took two books with him on his travels across Tasmania during the early years of the nineteenth century. One of them was the Bible, which is why the state now has the Walls of Jerusalem, Herods Gate, Lake Salome, Solomons Jewels, Damascus Gate and the Pool of Bethesda.

And the other was *The Arabian Nights*, which is why Tasmania has Bagdad and the Jordan River.

KOONTHAPAREE

'A place where men die.'

MOLE CREEK

As coincidence would have it, the number of moles in Mole Creek, in Tasmania's Upper Mersey Valley, precisely matches the number of moles in the rest of the state.

This number is, of course, zero.

Mole Creek's name probably comes from the way it, at one point, flows underground for a bit, and then comes up again, just like a mole.

MONSTER CREEK

Some people find Tasmania easy to ignore and I don't mind saying I'm one of them.

In 1962, however, it had everyone's attention. 'The world was stunned' at the news that the remains of a 'monster' had been found on a remote Tassie beach, the inlet to which was later dubbed Monster Creek.

'It was estimated to weigh at least nine tonnes, was six metres long and five and a half metres wide, had a very strong smell and appeared to be covered in a fine, wool-like coating.'

Responding to a 'frenzy of interest' from 'the international media', the Tasmanian government sent a bevy of experts to investigate the remains . . . which, in the event, didn't take very long.

It was a hunk of blubber from a whaling ship.

Hobart

Good news, residents of Hobart: your city's name means 'bright and shining intellect'. Or possibly 'bright and shining heart': no-one seems to agree. It's in the same word family as names like Hubert and Hubbard – a family that must have been kicked off by some Anglo-Saxon whose parents thought he was pretty hot stuff.

But what about Lord Robert Hobart, the man after whom Hobart was named? Was *he* hot stuff?

Well, he doesn't have a very bright and shining biography. England's Secretary of State for War and the Colonies at the time Tasmania was colonised, this soldier-turned-politician may have had an interesting personality but, if so, he kept it to himself. I can report that he was a soldier for a while, then an MP for a bit, and then became a privy councillor and the governor of Madras. In 1798, he inherited the Earldom of Buckinghamshire, entered the House of Lords and took charge of the colonies. And that's about all I can tell you, really, unless you want to hear all about the time he was joint postmaster-general and on the Board of Control for Indian Affairs . . .

Oh, hang on: two fun details – Hobart was married to Eleanor, the daughter of the first Baron Auckland, another blah British polly who lent his name to a town. And he died at the age of 55 after somehow managing to fall off his horse.

Collins Street David Collins, Lieutenant-Governor of Van Diemen's Land, 1804–10

Constitution Dock Opened in 1850, the same week that a new constitution came into effect

Davey Street Thomas Davey, Lieutenant-Governor of Van Diemen's Land, 1811–17

Elizabeth Street Elizabeth Macquarie, wife of Lachlan, NSW governor, 1810–21

Franklin Wharf Sir John Franklin, Van Diemen's Land governor, 1837–43

Mount Nelson David Nelson, botanist on the Bounty and 'the first white man on it'

Queens Domain A gift from Queen Victoria

Risdon Cove William Bellamy Risdon, second officer on board the ship which 'discovered' it

Rosny Point Lookout Named after Maximilien de Bethune, duc de Sully, of Rosny-sur-Seine in France

Runnymede The name of the Thames-side water meadow where the Magna Carta was signed

St David's Cathedral After a sixth-century saint in hilly Wales who miraculously created another hill

Salamanca Market The site, in Spain, of a major British victory during the Napoleonic wars

Sullivans Cove John Sullivan, Colonial Office undersecretary, 1801–04

The Tench Short for 'the penitentiary' or prison

MOUNT HORROR

There's a fascinating story about Mount Horror, a hill in Tasmania's north-east involving 'a madman with a penchant for decapitation'.

Unfortunately, it's also a false story. 'Horror' is just a corruption of 'Horitz'.

NORTH WEST BAY

Well, this is obviously a bay in the north-west of Tasmania, right?

Wrong, my friend. So, so wrong. North West Bay is actually in Tamania's south-east. Though I suppose it's still north-west of *something*.

NOWHERE ELSE

'All roads lead to Rome' is one of those sayings that's simply untrue. Some roads lead to Melbourne, for example, while others take you to Sydney and Perth.

And then we have a tiny dirt road half-hidden by trees that can be found on Tasmania's remote northern coast. Travel east on it and you'll eventually reach Sheffield, though why you'd want to go *there*, I really don't know.

That tiny town may be the best available option, however, because to the road's west there is Nowhere Else.

OUSE RIVER

I really don't want to be petty, but the sad fact is that I am. Named after one of the many Ouse rivers in the Mother Country, Tasmania's Ouse River has the same problem as all of them: 'ouse' is an Old English word meaning 'water'.

'Water River'? I mean, *come on*. What else would be in it? Pepsi?

PIEMAN RIVER

'Man's flesh is delicious, far better than fish or pork.'

Not my observation, I hasten to add. It came from one Alexander Pearce. The only convict to escape Hells Gates prison twice, Pearce was not a man you'd want to take on a camping trip – or at least, not if provisions were low. Both escape attempts eventually saw Pearce murder and eat his fellow escapees, for 'no man can tell what he would do when driven by hunger'.

Neither attempt, however, took place near the Pieman River. Long thought to have been named for Pearce's nickname, 'the Pieman', we know that it was named after one Thomas Kent, a convict who had previously worked as a pastry cook.

PORT DAVEY

'Be not afraid of greatness,' advises someone or other in *Twelfth Night*. 'Some are born great, some achieve greatness and some have greatness thrust upon them'.

But this person, whose name I must remember to look up, clearly forgot a fourth category: the 'some' who have greatness thrust upon them, and then airily let it drop to the floor.

And it is in this category that we can find Thomas Davey. A one-time soldier turned full-time drinker, he was 'indolent', 'dissipated in his manner and morals', 'expensive in his habits', 'thoughtless and volatile' and lacking in 'dignity'.

But on the other hand, he was friends with a cabinet minister. In 1811, therefore, the man after whom Port Davey is named was made governor of Van Diemen's Land. And in 1813, he finally arrived there. With him was his wife, a woman he'd tried to leave behind, but who had somehow boarded the ship. 'Upon being informed of her arrival Davey lost his temper and hurled his wig at the wall.'

He was also accompanied by debt. A 'resident' at the Gentleman's Prison for Debtors, Davey had hoped to give this particular landlord the slip, but the law followed him all the way to New Holland. His pay as governor of £800 per year was stopped by the authorities until the debt was settled . . . but he somehow still managed to live well.

Question marks about his handling of public finances eventually led to Davey's removal from the post, and his return to England.

His wife stayed behind.

QUEER KNOB

According to a travel blog, Tasmania boasts such attractions as Old Guys Dirty Hole, Tittee Gee Creek and, for some reason,

Boomers Bottom. According to Google Maps, however, it does not, which I must say seems like a pity.

The state can, however, boast a Robbins Passage (a waterway once visited by a sailor called Robbins) and some perky hills known as The Nipples. There's also a Funny Knob Creek not all that far from Queer Knob, and a Lake Fanny near Mossy Nipple Bend.

ROCKY HILLS

Want to know what's odd about the name 'Rocky Hills'?

The answer is: nothing at all. These little mountains near Swansea are indeed quite rocky, in the same way as Burnie's Round Hill is in fact rather round.

Much the same logic applies in Tasmania's Red Hills and Black Hills, while if you think about it carefully – and please take your time – you may be able to infer a thing or two about Flowery Gully and the presence of gravel on Gravelly Beach.

Other imaginative Tasmania place names include Mountain Field, Boat Harbour, Four Mile Creek and Meadowbank. And Saltwater River. And Sandy Bay. But since none of us is getting any younger, I propose we end things there.

TANINA

'To fart.'

THUNDER AND LIGHTNING BAY

I once had a girlfriend who got a bit cross sometimes, and then stayed cross for several days. Wobberertee, a daughter of the chief of the Plangermaireener nation, was apparently much the same. Her name roughly translates as 'Thunder and Lightning' and I think you can guess where she lived.

TOMAHAWK

The town of Tomahawk isn't shaped like a tomahawk, and nor is any feature nearby. But for some reason somebody named it that, and I'd be very grateful if you could let me know why.

TRIAL HARBOUR

As a safe place to park your boat for a bit, Trial Harbour is about on par with an erupting volcano, or perhaps the city of Hiroshima in 1945.

Ludicrously exposed to the elements – not least, the wild winds of the Roaring Forties – it is a place of giant swells and twisting squalls and hidden rocks and not much water. 'You soon learn if this place is for you,' says one hardy resident, who has had her windows smashed by a howling gale. 'Some people do pack their bags pretty quick, though.'

No longer used as a harbour, the bay got its name from a ship called the *Trial* that was once anchored there . . . and sank in a storm.

TROUSERS POINT

There is no real excuse for naming a place 'Trousers Point', but according to one website, there are 'a couple of possible explanations'.

'One story says the name commemorates the lucky escape by a certain Richard Burgess, without his trousers, from the wreck of the *Sarah Ann Blanche*. Another story assigns the name to the discovery of a box of trousers which had floated away and washed up on the beach from another wreck, that of the *Cambridgeshire* in 1875.'

Western Australia

About 71 per cent of the Earth is covered by water. Strictly between you, me and the lamppost, this means that 71 per cent of it looks more or less the same. Once they'd sailed out of sight of the land, in other words, ye olde seafarers couldn't just glance around and say, 'France is fifty miles that way', or 'That water looks Norwegian: full steam ahead!'

No sir. They had to rely on latitude and longitude.

Working out your latitude has always been easy enough. A bit like two archery targets placed back-to-back, lateral lines are two groups of parallel, concentric circles that rise and fall from the equator. You can work out how far north or south you are from the nearest one with a quick glance at the sun.

The lines of longitude, on the other hand, spread out from the North Pole like a demented spider's web, and get back together at some point in the South Pole. In the meantime, they all curve in a wildly *un*-parallel way, which makes measuring how far east and west you have travelled a tiny bit of a tricky task.

But in the early 1700s, it was essentially impossible. A sailor could be under the impression that he was somewhere near Africa, and then suddenly hit the Western Australia coast.

And, indeed, many sailors did. Western Australia place names like Dirk Hartog Island, Pelsaert Island, Cape Leeuwin, the Houtman Abrolhos and the Zuytdorp Cliffs all commemorate Dutch ships that drifted a little too far east on their way to the Spice Islands.

Other sailors came to Western Australia deliberately, most notably Willem de Vlamingh (who named Rottnest Island and the Swan River), and England's William Dampier (who named Shark Bay). Both explorers, however, found 'New Holland' to be a bit of a dry, barren dump, with the result that their governments decided to stay away, and Western Australia very nearly became French. Esperance, Geographe Bay and Cape Naturaliste were all named after Napoleonic ships which sailed by in the early 1800s to see if this remote desert was a place worth colonising.

We'll never know what they might have done, because the mere fact that the French were interested meant that their traditional enemies became interested too. The British formally took possession at King George Sound (a place near Albany, which they named after George's son).

And in 1829, they went the whole hog, renaming 'New Holland' Western Australia, and sending in the soldiers to make sure it wasn't changed back.

One such soldier was Captain James Stirling. After checking out the land around the Swan River – land that had recently been claimed for Britain by a Captain Charles *Fremantle* – he lobbied family friend and colonial secretary Sir George Murray to let him start a colony there. Eventually named 'Perth' after Murray's electorate in Perthshire (though Stirling is said to have preferred 'Hesperia', which means 'land of the west'), the Swan River colony essentially became Stirling's own personal fiefdom, after he was made its governor in 1831.

The Perth suburb of Stirling and the Stirling Ranges reflect this power, though he also had the good sense to name Mount Eliza after the then New South Wales governor's wife. Later governors also got in on the act, when the colony established towns like Broome, Northampton and Geraldton (Frederick Broome, John Hampton, Charles Fitzgerald) and 'discovered' natural features like the Ord River, Kennedy Range and Mount Weld (Harry Ord, Arthur Kennedy, Frederick Weld).

The explorers got a certain amount of credit too, to be fair, which is why Western Australia has places like Grey, Bunbury, Port Gregory and Mount Giles, together with Warburton, the Eyre Highway and Forrestfield.

But the bulk of West Australian place names are, of course, Indigenous. While it's unclear how many people lived in the state before settlement – one recent estimate is about 60000 – there is no shortage of places like Perenjori, Pithara and Pantapin, and lots of people are doing their best to work out what they all mean.

'We can't even be sure the Aboriginal names that exist now are spelt correctly or even in fact relate to local Aboriginal culture or language,' says the director of the Australian National Placenames Survey. 'Some, of course, may never be known because the original meanings have been lost forever with the obliteration of so many Aboriginal nations' language and cultures.'

But on a lighter note, we do know what at least *some* Indigenous and non-Indigenous West Australian place names mean. And quite a few of them are pretty funny.

ABROLHOS ISLANDS

There are many benefits to learning another language, but avoiding death probably ranks near the top.

A chain of 122 tiny islands, jagged rocks and submerged coral reefs, the Abrolhos Islands have hosted a crazy number of shipwrecks over the years, from the *Batavia*, the *Zeewijk* and the *Hadda*, to the *Marten*, the *Ocean Queen* and the *Windsor*.

If only just one of the men on board these ships had taken the time to learn Portuguese. 'Abrolhos' means 'spiked obstructions'.

ANKATELL

Founding a successful colony takes a pinch of luck, and at least one small-to-medium-sized brain.

Thomas Peel Junior seems to have had neither of these things. The first cousin of an English prime minister, and a deeply unpopular student at his posh public school, this 'difficult personality' received an early inheritance from his father, on the condition that he leave England and spend it elsewhere.

In 1828, Peel came up with the idea of founding a settlement at Swan River. The government granted him 250000 acres of land in what's now called Perth so long as he met certain conditions.

In the months that followed, he essentially failed to meet any of them, though he *did* manage to rack up a great deal of debt. Peel's 400 settlers arrived late, just in time for winter, and without much in the way of crops, food or tools. Peel also forgot to bring along any money or people with farming skills, and lost what supplies he *did* bring by insisting that a ship sail in bad weather. Many settlers died in the years that followed, and the ones that didn't soon abandoned the colony.

Their memory, however, lives on in Ankatell, a suburb Peel named after a friend.

BEACON ISLAND

A 'beacon,' according to dictionary.com, is 'a lighthouse, signal buoy, etc., on a shore or at a dangerous area at sea to warn and guide vessels'.

While Beacon Island may well have such an apparatus today, it was clearly missing back in 1629, when the *Batavia* tried to sail by. Some 40 crew members are thought to have drowned when that Dutch ship hit a reef, but that still left over 200 able to make it to shore.

The *Batavia*'s captain then set off in a dinghy to get help from Jakarta, leaving a former pharmacist called Jeronimus Cornelisz in charge.

When the captain returned some three months later, with more men and a big new ship, he was greeted with scenes straight out of a horror movie. Around 120 corpses lay buried on Beacon Island: some drowned, some strangled, some bludgeoned, and quite a few hacked into little red bits.

It turned out that when supplies on the small island had started to run out – all traces of hope vanishing with them – Cornelisz had assembled a gang of 40 men and given them instructions to kill everyone else. The few children on board were among the many murdered, though most of the women were kept alive, as sex slaves.

BIDAMINOCK

'A place which is haunted by the evil spirits of the dead.' So, houses going cheap.

BIG DICK BORE

A bore, as we know, is a sort of deep, round pit from which things like water or gas can be pumped.

I don't know why Big Dick Bore in Kalgoorlie is so named, but let's hope it involves someone called Richard.

BUNGLE BUNGLES

Somebody bungled when they wrote down Bungle Bungles. The mountain range should really be 'Bundle Bundle', the name of a local grass.

BURSWOOD

Technically speaking, the Perth suburb of Burswood ought to be spelled with two 'r's, having been named after Burrswood in Kent.

Remember that, next time you go to Burswood Casino. Or better still, don't go at all.

BUSSELTON

Imagine that you were a farmer in south-western Australia and that, one day, a few cattle strayed. If you finally tracked them down to a hitherto unknown piece of land, and decided it was actually *so* nice you might just buy it, would you proceed to give said land a name like 'Cattle Chosen'?

I hope and pray that the answer is 'no', but such was the story of Mr John Bussell.

Name-wise, that farmer's work does not end there: 'Cattle Chosen' is just one of many marks he left on the Western Australia map. You can also visit Gracetown (named after John's daughter), and the Margaret River (one of his cousins).

Even the Capel River owes its name to one Capel Bussell, another member of the busy brood.

CAPE INSCRIPTION

Personally, I would have thought that if your name was 'Dirk Hartog', you might consider this information best kept to yourself.

But apparently Dirk disagreed. When the Dutch sea captain of that name became the first European to see Western Australia, he did his best to make sure everyone knew.

His 'best', in this instance, involved inscribing his name and the date on a big pewter plate, attaching said plate to a plank, and putting said plank on a prominent cliff. Eighty-one years later, miraculously enough, yet another Dutch seaman saw the plate, and replaced it with one of his own.

And then a third ship came along. While this one was French, its policy was still quite pro-plate: Captain Jacques Hamelin of the *Naturaliste* added an inscription of his own in 1801, and while he was at it, gave the place a new name.

CHRISTMAS HILLS

Jolly name for a town, yes?

Sorry, but the answer is no. The 'Christmas' here does not refer to yuletide cheer, with its turkeys and presents and puddings, but to a shepherd by the name of David Christmas, who could have done with a map and a compass. David got lost in 1842, and it was in these hills his corpse was found.

COCKBURN

Named after Sir George Cockburn, a distinguished seaman.

COOLIBULLUP

'Infested with kangaroo ticks.'

CROOKED BROOK

This brook is bendy, not dishonest. Or, at least, so I'm led to believe.

CYANIDE SWAMP

No, this Kalgoorlie swamp does not contain cyanide. But one suspects that the water's not great.

DAMBORING

Being about 200 kilometres north-east of Perth – that is, slap-bang in the middle of the desert – this patch of land probably *is* damn boring, but that's not how it came by the name. 'Dam' and 'boring' are local words meaning something like 'rocks' and 'lake'.

DAMPIER

The town of Dampier gets its name from William Dampier, a pirate-turned-explorer-turned-travel-writer who was the first Englishman to ever visit our shores.

But I'm not sure if he would really appreciate the tribute. One of the reasons that it took England another 100 years to dispatch Captain Cook southwards was that Dampier was so unimpressed. 'The land is of a dry sandy soil, destitute of water,' he wrote of New Holland, a hot, barren desert that he felt must house 'the most miserable wretches in the universe'.

'The woods are not thick, nor the trees very big,' he wrote of his 12 days in Western Australia's (admittedly grim) north-west in the 1697 bestseller, *A Voyage Around the World*. In among the 'troublesome' flies and 'unpleasing natives', Dampier 'saw no trees that bore fruit or berries' and 'neither was the sea very plentifully stored with fish'.

And that's about it, really. Australia gets about a quarter of a chapter in a book that has 20, and every word is some kind of whine.

DINGO KNOB

A small hill occasionally visited by dingos.

DISAPPOINTMENT HILL

Frank Hann was a thirsty man, back in the summer of 1903. So like Jack and Jill, he went up a hill in order to fetch a pail of water. And while he didn't fall down (much less break his crown), he also found cause to frown. Disappointment Hill, you see, was entirely dry; you won't find water, no matter how hard you try.

DISASTER WATER

While dogs are a man's best friend, desert explorers by and large prefer camels. Losing one is inconvenient, and losing two is a disaster.

When such a disaster struck at a remote West Australian well, Nathaniel Buchanan decided to let the world know. Why suffer in silence when you can suffer for all time on a map?

EMU CREEK

Emus are all over Australia, so it's no surprise they're all over our maps. Our wide, brown land boasts Emu Flats and Emu Fields, an Emu Ridge and an Emu Bay. There are Emu Plains and Emu Parks and, of course, there's an Emu Creek.

What *is* a little surprising, however, is that there was also an Emu *War*. Much like the nomadic barbarians who were forever threatening the borders of Ancient Rome, the world's second-largest bird likes to travel in big, angry packs. After the long, hot summer in 1932, roughly 20 000 of them descended on the Campion district, and started to eat all the freshly grown wheat.

This would not do, Australia's defence minister decided, and promptly sent in the troops to defend all the farms. Armed with state-of-the-art Lewis machine guns, a crack unit from the Royal Australian Artillery arrived and proceeded to show the emus who's boss.

Unfortunately, it turned out that the emus were boss. When the troops opened fire, the birds simply dodged. Then had some more wheat. And then dodged again. While about a dozen of them died, and a few sustained injuries, that still left roughly 19 980 birds entirely at liberty, and in every way still enjoying their breakfast.

'If we had a military division with the bullet-carrying capacity of these birds,' a Major Meredith later reflected, 'it could face any army in the world. They face machine guns with the invulnerability of tanks.'

Less than a week after the 'Emu War' had begun, the defence minister ordered a retreat.

FREMANTLE

Admiral Sir Charles Howe Fremantle GCB RN was a man with many letters after his name.

But the ones that interest me are r-a-p-i-s-t. The second son of a baronet, Fremantle was a low-ranking 26-year-old naval officer when he was charged with the rape of a 15-year-old servant.

The penalty for this was death. But, being blue-blooded, Charles got a promotion. His father's well-connected friend, the Marquess of Buckingham, paid off the two witnesses and used his influence to lean on the judiciary.

But it wasn't quite enough to 'get rid of the evidence'. Charles had to get out as well. Swiftly receiving a promotion to captain, he sailed south in the spring of 1828 to claim Australia's west coast for King George. Several months later he found it, and dutifully hoisted a flag at the mouth of the Swan.

And just three months later, he was out of there (though he did once return, for a week). Fremantle ended his days in comfort in England, as an admiral and knight of the realm.

No-one knows what happened to the servant girl. But I suspect it wasn't good.

GEEKABEE HILL

Not far from the also-odd Twongkup Reserve, Geekabee Hill's somewhat unusual name is said to have come from the initials of Mr George Kershaw Brown.

GIBSON DESERT

Some time in the summer of 1874, the well-known explorer Ernest Giles decided it was time that he explored a bit more. Western Australia's vast deserts were his target this time, and just as he was about to set off (as he later recalled in his memoir), he was 'accosted by a short young man' who said 'My name's Alf Gibson, and I want to go out with you.'

'I said, "Well, can you shoe? Can you ride? Can you starve? Can you go without water? And how would you like to be speared by the blacks outside?" He said he could do everything I had mentioned, and he wasn't afraid of the blacks. He was not a man I would have picked out of a mob, but men were scarce, and as he seemed so anxious to come, and as I wanted somebody, I agreed to take him.'

What Giles *should* have asked, in hindsight, was 'Can you navigate?' At one point during the expedition, you see, he gave the young Gibson a horse and asked him to fetch some water from a nearby creek. It was the last time anyone ever saw him – but not the last time they mentioned his name. Somewhere in the Gibson Desert there lie the bones of an Alfred Gibson.

HUTT RIVER

When it comes to bald, boring statements of fact, no-one does it better than a bureaucrat. 'In 1970, a Western Australian farmer re-named his property "Hutt River Province" in a unilateral declaration of independence,' says the Australian government website. 'The Australian Government does not legally or otherwise recognise the so-called Hutt River Province.'

Hidden behind these bland words is a gloriously bizarre story. It saw a renegade wheat farmer decide to call himself 'Prince Leonard' and declare his wheat farm a sovereign realm. Hutt River's handful of 'citizens' continue to use their own currency and print their own passports, pay their own taxes and pass their own laws. At one point, they even declared war.

All of which makes it somewhat ironic that Hutt River was named after a loyal MP.

INNALOO

Named after a local woman, this inner Perth suburb is almost as good for a giggle as the nearby Upper Swan.

INTERCOURSE ISLAND

Captain Phillip Parker King enjoyed regular intercourse with most of his crew. Intercourse was also a feature of his relationships with his friends – and, of course, with his family too.

By 'intercourse' I obviously mean 'talking', and so did Phillip when he named Intercourse Island. It was there, about 1500 kilometres north of Perth, that the explorer encountered some Aborigines, and enjoyed a pleasant chat.

ISRAELITE BAY

Foreskins are a big part of the Bible. The good book mentions the little suckers at least 22 times – most famously in Samuel 18:25, when young David (of statue, star and Goliath fame) is asked to go to war with a rival tribe. King Saul tells him to come back with at least 100 of their foreskins, but David does better and chops off twice that.

Impressive stuff, I'm sure you'll agree, particularly as we can be sure that he didn't cheat. As Israelites, David and his men would have all been circumcised, so there was no easy way to bulk up their haul.

Circumcision, of course, is common all over the world. It was even big in the Great Australian Bight. According to Norman Tindale, the author of *Aboriginal Tribes of Australia*, 'the European name of Israelite Bay is a geographical label witness to this being the boundary between those [tribes] who did and did not practice circumcision.'

JINGALUP

If you've ever got a spare couple of hours, and absolutely no interest in having a good time, you could sit down with a map and a coffee, and work out how many West Australian place names end in '-up'.

Here's a small sample, to help get you started: Mariginiup, Boilup, Badgebup, Carrolup, Dwellingup, Jerdacuttup.

Still with me? Then here are some more: Coodanup, Coolbellup, Boyanup, Cowaramup, Cooloongup, Jerramungup, Jingalup.

Don't worry, I'm nearly done here. Cardup, Wonnerup, Burekup, Yallingup and Karrinyup.

Okay, stopping now. And if you're wondering why there are so many of the suckers, the boring answer is that 'up' means 'land'.

JINNERBEEKER

'Bad feet.'

JUKEMERING

'Kangaroo thighs.'

KIMBERLEY

It would be nice to think that this beautiful part of the world was named after a beautiful woman.

But it would also be wrong. The north-west bit of Western Australia gets its name from Lord Wodehouse, the first Earl of Kimberley and a former secretary of state for the colonies.

LUCKY BAY

The 'discoverers' of the different parts of Western Australia didn't always seem that impressed with their finds. The state's coast abounds with dispirited-sounding names like Hopeless Reach and Disaster Bay. False Entrance is fairly close to Disappointment Loop, while anyone considering a trip to Cape Naturaliste should know that it was once Cape Discontent.

It's nice, then, to know that at least one explorer liked to think positive. Lucky Bay received its name from Matthew Flinders in 1802, after he anchored there navigating a 'hazardous . . . labyrinth of islands and rocks' at night during 'strong southwest winds'.

'The critical circumstance under which this place was discovered induced me to give it the name of Lucky Bay.'

MAIRMUDDING

'I will spear you.'

MERRYGINING

'A place frequented by an evil spirit.'

MONKEY MIA

One of Western Australia's oddest place names, 'Monkey Mia' may also be its most obscure. A nature reserve north-east of Denham, it could be named after a schooner called the *Monkey* which passed through Shark Bay in 1834.

Though having said that, another boat called the *Herald* is said to have had a monkey as a mascot when it surveyed the bay a few decades later. And monkeys certainly weren't an unknown pet among the Malay pearlers who occasionally camped nearby.

But going on the theory that the dullest explanation is usually the right one, I'm betting it's a corruption of a local Indigenous word – there's a not dissimilar one which means 'saltwater'.

MOOGENALLIN

'A peculiar smell.'

MOUNT DESTRUCTION

'The explorer does not make the country, he must take it as he finds it. And though to the discoverer of the finest regions the greatest applause is awarded, it should be borne in mind that the difficulties of traversing such a country cannot be nearly so great as those which confront the less fortunate traveller, who finds himself surrounded by heartless deserts.'

Ernest Giles, the explorer who said these words, knew a great deal about heartless deserts. He spent his career walking around Western Australia, looking for fertile pastures and, of course, finding none.

With his uncanny knack for finding places that were dry, hot and barren, it's no surprise Giles headed in the direction of Mount Destruction in early 1874, when his party looked like dying of thirst. As you might have guessed, it was as dry as a bone, with the result that four horses passed away.

At this, Giles gave up and began the long journey home. First, though, he gave the hill an appropriate name, 'for the visit to it had destroyed alike my horses and my hopes.'

MOUNT KOKEBY

This tiny town in the West Australian wheatbelt was actually named after the sixth Baron *Rokeby*. But when a train station was built there, and some chump accidentally wrote 'Kokeby' on the timetable, it was considered easier to just rename the town.

MOUNT MEHARRY

Would you believe that this mountain was named after an instruction given to a man called Harry? A Harry who was so granite-jawed, pert-bottomed, big-muscled and flat-stomached that someone ordered him into her (or his) bed?

No? Well, that's okay because it isn't true. Western Australia's highest mountain was instead named after a William Meharry, the state's chief geodetic surveyor back in the '50s.

(Another reason to love the name is that Gina Rinehart doesn't, by the way. She's twice now applied to have it renamed Mount Hancock, after her magnate dad.)

MOWBRDONEMARGODINE

'Where the wombats fight.'

NIAGARA

The Niagara Falls are a natural wonder. Straddling the border between Canada and the United States, they have the highest flow rate of any waterfall in the world, and a combined drop of over 165 feet (50 metres). About 4 million cubic feet of water (over 113 million litres) fall to their floor *every minute*, in front of millions of tourists a year.

The Niagara waterfall in Western Australia, on the other hand, is not a natural wonder. Found near the town of Niagara (which subsequently adopted its tongue-in-cheek name), it's about 10 feet (3 metres) tall when it's been raining a lot. But that hasn't happened for quite a while.

NILLUP

According to Mrs Rose Watson of the Augusta Historical Society, Nillup got its name from a 'popular local identity' who preferred to hide his light under a bushel. Harold Pullin eventually agreed to lend his name to the town, so long as they spelled it backwards.

NOMANS LAKE

While it's been on the map since at least 1892, no man knows what 'Nomans' means, and most women are pretty vague on it too. The best guess is that since the lake was in such a remote and empty region, it essentially belonged to no man.

NORSEMAN

A horse is a horse, of course, of course, and so, it turns out, is a Norse.

The gold fields town of Norseman got its name from a horse called Hardy Norseman, who got his hoof caught in a rock. When his owner hopped off to lend him a hand, he discovered that the rock was a rich, gleaming yellow – or, to be more precise, gold. Hardy Norseman had uncovered a giant gold reef and, in doing so, founded a town.

NORTHAMPTON

Competition for jobs in the early days of the colonies was not always quite as fierce as it should have been. When John Hampton was fired from his job overseeing the convicts in Van Diemen's Land, it was not only because of allegations of cruelty, but because – by employing 'convict labour for personal profit' – he was also clearly corrupt.

But this did not stop him getting another job. As, um, governor of Western Australia. 'Somewhat tyrannical and harsh' and prone to behave 'like the white overseer of a slave plantation', he quickly set convicts to work on a palatial governor's mansion. And a palatial governor's holiday house, on Rottnest Island.

When the comptroller-general of the Convict Department resigned in protest, the governor replaced him with George Hampton. His, um, son.

NORTH POLE

A site of great scientific interest, the North Pole boasts some big black rocks that may date back billions of years.

What makes these rocks more interesting than, well, rocks, is that all of them are in some sense *alive*. A collection of single-celled microbes, it was 'stromatolites' such as these that started life on Earth, and helped produce all the oxygen you and I need to survive. North Pole in the Pilbara is one of only five places on the planet where these primitive life forms can still be found.

But that's no reason to call the place 'Stromatolite', or some other relevant thing, when you could instead go with a gag. North Pole got its ironic name because the weather there can get pretty hot.

OPHTHALMIA RANGE

If you're going to trek through the desert, you need a good pair of legs. But good eyes are important as well.

In 1876, the explorer Ernest Giles took it upon himself to walk all the way from central South Australia to Perth – and then, even more idiotically, walk all the way back. As well as sunburn and back pain and God knows what else, he not unnaturally contracted trachoma in the course of his travels,

Perth

Perth may not be a particularly good name for a city, but for Sir George Murray, that didn't particularly matter. Best known in his day for an affair with a married woman and today for a river which he never went near, Murray was an MP for Perthshire, and a man who knew how to rack up the votes.

With a general election looming the following year, he used his position as Secretary of the Colonies to propose that Britain's next colony, in Western Australia, be built around a town with a name like, say, Perth. 'By his lavish patronage of relations and friends in Perthshire, [the new colony also] gained some third-rate public servants.'

The approach certainly helped him to keep his seat, but he needed more help than that to hang on to his job. Fired in 1830, after just two years in the role, Murray was dubbed 'indolent', 'feeble' and 'a failure' who 'allowed his under-secretaries to do all the business and govern him'.

His 'countenance and natural stateliness and simple dignity of demeanour were all that can be desired in a Secretary of State,' another colleague acidly remarked, 'if to look the character were the one thing needful'. He 'had never met with any public officer so inefficient'.

Cottesloe Beach *The 1st Baron Cottesloe, brother of Admiral Sir Charles Fremantle*

Elizabeth Quay *Queen Elizabeth II*

Hay Street *Robert William Hay, Permanent Undersecretary of State for the Colonies, 1825–36*

Heirisson Island *Thought to be the name of an early explorer*

King Street *King William IV*

Kings Park *King Edward VII*

Kwinana Freeway *'Young woman'*

Langley Park *TW Langley, Acting Lord Mayor*

Murray Street *Sir George Murray, Secretary of State for War and the Colonies, 1928–30*

Point Belches *Peter Belches, Third Lieutenant on board HMS Success*

Scarborough Beach *Named after Scarborough, a beach resort in Yorkshire*

Wellington Square *The Duke of Wellington*

– a painful eye condition that's also known as 'ophthalmia' or 'the sandy blight'.

'My eyes had been so bad all day, I was in agony, [and] at length I couldn't see at all,' he later wrote of the day he came upon 'a range of rounded hills' which he called 'Ophthalmia Range'.

'In consequence of my suffering so much . . . I could not take any observations, and I cannot be very certain where this range lies.' (It is in fact about 1200 kilometres north of Perth.)

PINK LAKE

No rhetorical flourishes here, people: Pink Lake near the town of Esperance belongs in the same category as the Great Sandy Desert, Big Grove and Brown Hill. In certain sorts of weather, its water really *does* turn pink, thanks to some strange sort of algae.

POINT TORMENT

The best-known passenger to ever sail on the *Beagle* was a naturalist named Charles Darwin. His five-year voyage to the Galapagos Islands famously inspired the theory of evolution (which, whatever creationists might tell you, is also a fact).

Before Darwin came on board, however, the *Beagle* went to Western Australia. And the crew's view of animals was not quite as warm. 'A name was soon found for our new territory,' wrote Captain Stokes, after a less-than-successful trip to Port

Torment. 'With rueful unanimity, we conferred [the name upon it because of] the incessant and vindictive . . . swarms of mosquitoes who had evidently been resolved to give the newcomers a warm welcome.'

QUINNINUP

'Plenty of rats.'

ROTTNEST ISLAND

Name-wise, Rottnest Island got off to a pretty good start, but it's been downhill ever since. For millennia it was known as 'Wadjemup', the 'place across the water where the spirits are'. And when an English ship sailed by in 1681, it became the equally pleasant-sounding 'Maiden's Isle'.

Nowadays, however, the island is named after the Dutch word for 'rat's nest' – and, even worse, gets called 'Rotto' for short. When a Captain Willem de Vlamingh camped there in 1695, it would seem that he saw dozens of quokkas and naturally assumed they were rats.

SECRET HARBOUR

Secret Harbour isn't exactly a secret, being part of a city of over 2 million. And technically speaking, it's not really a harbour: just a Perth suburb straddling the coast.

So what's with the name? It apparently dates back to two businessmen, who planned to build a big marina there in the

1980s, with a big (yet 'secret') harbour for the super-rich. When the government scrapped the proposal in favour of building a brand new suburb, some bureaucrat mysteriously decided that there was no need to scrap the name.

SCENTED KNOB

A largish mountain with sweet-smelling flowers.

SUBIACO

Are you okay with your 'lustful urges'? St Benedict wasn't.

Horrified by the brothel- and booze-filled culture of ancient Rome, this pure-minded young student left the city in about 500AD, in order to spend three years living alone in a cave.

Known as Subiaco because it was 'below a lake', said cave was also surrounded by thorny brambles – brambles which Ben found useful whenever a bestial urge struck. Rather than just give in and masturbate, or grit his teeth and think unsexy thoughts, he liked to strip naked and roll around in the thorns until the mood finally passed.

Such purity naturally won him admirers – and before long he had his own flock. The order of monks that St Benedict founded at Subiaco went on to have thousands of chapters all over the world. One such chapter moved to Perth. Can you guess where it was based?

SUCCESS

The HMS *Success* was not exactly a success on its first voyage to Western Australia.

Sent to bring supplies to the fledgling Swan River colony, that ship somehow managed to get stuck on a reef, about 10 kilometres from the shore. Towed in several weeks later, she was dismantled in the Perth suburb that now bears her misleading name.

Shout-outs to shipwrecks are a bit of a tradition, it would seem, when it comes to the West Australian coast. Rockingham,

Guilderton, Alkimos and Kwinana all got their (rather nice) names from boats that had a bad day.

TOBBERY

'Something dirty.'

TRYALL ROCKS

Much like the *Titanic*, the first voyage of the seventeenth-century trading ship the *Tryall* also ended up being its last.

Helmed by one Captain Brooke, a man who was not at his best with a compass, it sailed so far east from South Africa on its way to Indonesia that it accidentally hit the Australian coast.

And when I say hit, I really mean *hit*: it slammed straight into what are now the Tryall Rocks. Ninety-three men perished in what was essentially Australia's first shipwreck, though the ship's cargo of silver survived.

Leaping into a large, empty skiff as quickly as he could, while his crew screamed, struggled and drowned, the brave Captain Brooke managed to sail to Batavia, 1800 kilometres to the north. He proceeded to blame a faulty map for his failure, and say, 'Sorry, but all the silver sank.'

After returning to London, he was given command of another vessel, which, of course, he eventually sank.

USELESS LOOP

Every person is good at something, and the same goes for every place.

Useless Loop, about 800 kilometres north of Perth, was named by a Frenchman called de Freycinet who, like so many people, was a bit quick to judge. Having decided that the bay's big sandbar made it useless as a harbour, he gave it a name that said just that and sailed off in *un peu de huff.*

Nowadays, however, the bay is anything but useless. Not only can big ships dock there easily, they can all sail off with some world-class salt. Owned and operated by a Japanese company, Useless Loop is home to a giant evaporative solar farm that produces 1.6 million tonnes of salt every year.

WOLFE CREEK CRATER

There are no wolves at this tourist hot spot (let alone serial killers looking like John Jarratt). The meteorite crater made famous by the movie *Wolf Creek* actually got its name from a Mr Robert Wolfe, the owner of a small store nearby.

WOOP WOOP

Woop Woop may mean the middle of nowhere, but it's also the name of an abandoned mill town. It was not, perhaps, a name that signalled confidence about the town's future, and it would seem the lack of confidence was entirely well-placed.

XANTHIPPE

'By all means marry,' Socrates once advised an acolyte. 'If you get a good wife, you'll be happy. If you get a bad one, you'll become a philosopher.'

Needless to say, Socrates became a philosopher. A 'nagging shrew' with a ferocious temper, his aristocratic wife Xanthippe is said to have once grabbed a chamber-pot to pour over his head in a fit of rage. Also known to trample on his food and tear his clothes, she was, according to a contemporary, 'the hardest to get along with of all the women there are . . . or ever were . . . or ever will be.'

There's also a Xantippe in Western Australia, of course. Though the spelling has been slightly altered, it's said to have been named after that famously hard woman because of its granite-like ground.

ZUYTDORP CLIFFS

On 1 August 1711, a Dutch trading ship set off for Jakarta with a cargo of new silver coins. It was never seen again.

In 1927, however, some old silver coins were discovered on some Western Australian cliffs, along with some carved bits of timber. Could they have come from the *Zuytdorp*? Well, the area's now called the Zuytdorp Cliffs.

Like the *Batavia* before it, and many ships since, it would seem the Dutch ship accidentally sailed too far east, until a coral reef got in its way. Over the decades, divers have found cannonballs, anchors and a veritable 'carpet of silver' scattered around the sea floor at the foot of the cliff.

The *real* treasure, however, may be biological: some say that the sailors not only survived, but actually shacked up with the locals. And it's certainly true that a few English settlers centuries later wrote that Western Australian Aborigines often had lighter skin and fairly European features.

More interesting still, perhaps, is the fact that there's an extremely rare genetic condition called Ellis-van Creveld syndrome that is not actually all *that* rare in Western Australia. It was also not that rare in the Netherlands in the decade or so before 1711. In fact, it was 'rife'.

South Australia

As names go, 'South Australia' is not all that exciting (though I suppose you might say the same thing about the state). But things could have been worse, if the Dutch had had their way. When the *Gulden Zeepaerdt* sailed by in 1627, those on board saw the south coast of what they then knew as New Holland, and gave it the name 'Pieter Nuyts Land', after a prominent Dutch official.

Note that I did not say 'a nice Dutch official'. 'Haughty and domineering', this Nuyts is best remembered for his time as ambassador to Japan, where he earned a place for himself in Asian school textbooks as 'a typical arrogant western bully'. Eventually fired and gaoled for diddling the accounts, his other achievements included marrying a Taiwanese woman against her will, and enjoying dirty talk so much during his numerous affairs that he put a translator under his bed.

South Australia still has a Nuyts Archipelago but the 'Pieter Nuyts Land' name is long gone – as, indeed, are the Dutch.

For the next 174 years, South Australia was foreign-visitor-free, and then all of a sudden it got two lots at once. From the east came two French naval ships, under instructions from the little emperor to chart 'Terre Napoleon'. And from the west came Matthew Flinders, on his voyage around Terra Australis.

They bumped into each other in 1802, at a place that's now called Encounter Bay, but seem to have spent the rest of their time dotting the coastline with as many names as they possibly could. Fleurieu Peninsula, Lacepede Bay, Guichen Bay, D'Estrees Bay, Cape Du Couedic and Vivonne Bay are just some of the many French contributions to the South Australia coastline, while Flinders came up with a few like Kangaroo Island and Thorny Passage – and then let his superiors add a few dozen more.

'Very few names are applied by me,' he later wrote of this practice, 'for where I could not find a descriptive one, it was left to the Admiralty, or those whom their Lordships might chuse, to apply a name. It is not only consistent with propriety that the planners and promoters of a voyage of discovery should have a principle share in affixing names to the discovered parts, but it is necessary that the baptizing mania of some navigators should be under control, to prevent so many repetitions of names as we find in different parts of the world; nay, sometimes in the same part.'

Charles Sturt would have thought this was nonsense. The next explorer to visit South Australia (which was then still part of New South Wales), his 1829 journey to the mouth of the Murray resulted in a Sturt Stony Desert, a Sturt National Park and a Sturt River, plus a suburb, highway and football team that all sound a bit like 'turt'.

It also resulted in a glowing report on the land and its potential for settlement. 'My eye never fell on a country of more promising aspect, or more favourable position,' the explorer wrote to his superiors in the Colonial Office. 'It would appear that a spot has at last been found upon the south coast of New Holland to which the colonists might venture with every prospect of success.'

And venture they did. More than 600 settlers set sail from London in 1836 – and not a single one of them was a convict. A groundbreaking commercial project funded by private investors, South Australia was an entirely free colony in the American sense (that is, wealthy landowners exploiting cheap immigrants).

A Colonel Robert Torrens supervised the sale of land (which may help explain why that land now includes places such as the River Torrens, Lake Torrens, Torrensville and Torrens Park), while other shareholders in the venture included John Rundle, Charles Hindley, Raikes Currie, John Pirie and Henry Waymouth. All of their names are now found on the streets of Adelaide, a city that was named after England's then queen.

Those streets were laid out by a Colonel William Light (Light River, Colonel Light Gardens, Light Square), though the ultimate responsibility obviously rested with the colony's first chief, Governor John Hindmarsh . . . whose responsibilities included the suburb of Hindmarsh, Hindmarsh Square, Hindmarsh Island and the Hindmarsh Valley.

Later governors obviously got on the map too, in places like Jamestown, Daly Waters, Gawler and Robe, while some of them chose to honour their wives, with places like Port Augusta, Lucindale and Blanchetown.

But it was the new landowners (being, um, new landowners) who ended up naming a great deal of the land. It seems a safe bet that Allendale, Angaston, Charlestone and Normanville were once owned by rich but not necessarily very inventive men called Al, Gus, Chuck and Norm.

The colony wasn't all Chucks and Norms, however. South Australia's much-vaunted commitment to liberty sent immigrants flocking from all over the world. While the state has plenty of English and Scottish place names, like Hyde Park, Malvern and McLaren Vale, it also has a big heap of Irish ones, like the Clare Valley, Auburn and Armagh. Irish Catholics came flocking to the City of Churches during the nineteenth century, and plenty of Germans fleeing religious persecution came along in their wake. South Australia had no less than 69 German place names before World War I saw a great many ditched.

What else? Well, explorers of course. Mount Babbage, Mount Barker, Mount Burr, Baxter Cliffs, Lake Eyre, Cadell, Darke Peake, the Delisser Sandhills, Lake Frome and Horrocks Pass are all named after men who wandered the South Australian desert, trying and failing to find somewhere fertile. And, needless to say, there are plenty of Indigenous names – though how many of them are appropriate (or indeed coherent) is, as in other states, anyone's guess.

The final category is 'interesting names'. For more on them, just turn the page.

ADMELLA DUNES

Stand on the Admella Dunes these days and you won't see much beyond waves, sea and sand.

On 6 August 1859, however, you would have seen quite a bit. It was on that day that a steamship called the *Admella* got stuck on a reef, more or less a mile from the shore. Oh so slowly, it then started to break up, as men, women and children clung on.

Eight horrific days later, sad to report, 24 of them were still clinging on. They looked 'more like statues than human beings', according to the lifeboat captain who eventually came by. 'Their eyes [were] fixed, their lips were black for want of water, and their limbs were bleached white and swollen through exposure to the relentless surf.'

And what's worse, they were the lucky ones. Eighty-nine passengers drowned over the course of the week. Or died slowly, from dehydration and cold.

ALLIGATOR GORGE

No alligators here, I am pleased to report, though there was apparently once 'an Aboriginal shepherd named Alli who camped at the top of the range'.

BABAWALTHI

'Bad water.'

Adelaide

An obscure princess from Saxe-Meiningen, Adelheid Louise Therese Karolina Wilhelmina didn't expect fidelity when she married the King of England in 1818.

Which is good, because she didn't get it.

An obese alcoholic with 'crude and tactless manners', William IV already had ten illegitimate children with an actress, but he needed a legitimate heir. After negotiations with other blue-blooded candidates fell through, he had to settle on Adelheid, a highly religious girl 27 years his junior, whom he had never met. 'Her portraits show her as a charming looking woman, delicate and a little sad.'

'She is doomed, poor innocent creature, to become my wife,' William wryly said of his future spouse, who later changed her name to the more English 'Adelaide'.

She was also doomed, poor innocent creature, to be associated with Adelaide, a city whose site happened to be chosen on their 13th wedding anniversary, and so was given her name.

Beerenberg Farm *'Berry mountain'*

Belair National Park *Probably named after Bel Air in Martinique, the birthplace of a surveyor's wife*

Bonython Park *Sir John Bonython, long-time editor of the Adelaide Advertiser*

Cleland Conservation Park *Sir John Burton Cleland, distinguished professor of pathology at the University of Adelaide*

Henley Beach *Named after the English town of Henley-on-Thames*

Hindmarsh Square *Sir John Hindmarsh, South Australia governor, 1836–38*

Hurtle Square *Sir James Hurtle Fisher, Mayor of Adelaide, 1840–42, 1852–54*

King William Street *William IV*

Light Square *Colonel William Light, South Australia surveyor-general*

Mount Barker *Collet Barker, early explorer*

Rundle Mall *John Rundle, a British MP*

Rymill Park *Sir Arthur Rymill, Lord Mayor of Adelaide, 1950–54*

Victoria Square *Queen Victoria*

Whitmore Square *William Wolryche-Whitmore, a British MP*

BACKSTAIRS PASSAGE

Some people think that 'Backstairs Passage' is a ridiculous name and, personally, I think they're right.

For Matthew Flinders, however, it was a perfectly logical label for this alternative little path to the Fleurieu Peninsula.

BAGNALL WELL

Husbands cheat on their wives all the time, but it is a rare man who betrays his dog.

One man, however, probably should have. Bagnall Well is said to have got its name from a shepherd who was killed in 1851. He is said to have had a 'very savage dog which attacked the [local] Aborigines, who remonstrated with Bagnall without avail. As he would not kill the dog, they killed him' instead.

BAROSSA VALLEY

Properly spelled 'Barrosa', South Australia's famous wine region was named after a famous wine region in Spain.

But wine has nothing to do with the reason why. A surveyor gave the then-vineyard-free valley the name because one of his friends had fought in the Battle of Barrosa.

BASKET RANGE

Some people say that one of this timber town's very first residents was a licence inspector named Mr Basket. Others say the name commemorates a wife who brought her husband big baskets of lunch.

I say that, either way, Basket Range is a stupid name.

BAXTER RANGE

Lake Eyre could have been Lake Baxter, had Edward Eyre's fellow explorer known how to duck.

A one-time convict and heavy drinker, who had managed to turn himself into a 'most useful, well-behaved man', John Baxter was shot by two members of Eyre's expedition, so they could run away with what remained of the food.

'There can be little doubt that the remains found are those of poor Baxter,' wrote Edward Eyre, when he returned from a scouting trip to discover a corpse at what is now Baxter Range.

'No grave will be found as none was made; the circumstances of the moment and rocky nature of the ground precluded that. I could only leave my ill-fated companion covered over with a blanket where he fell, shot dead by one of the natives who accompanied me.'

BLOOD CREEK

Ready for a gruesome story?

Well, I'm afraid that you're not going to get one. Blood Creek was named after a Mr JHS Blood, who worked at a nearby telegraph office in the 1870s.

There probably *are* a few good stories about Doom Wall, Death Rock and Devils Peak, all South Australian crags that people like to climb, or Deadmans Dugout, a now defunct mine. But I have not, alas, uncovered any of them, which means that this entry should probably end now.

BOOBOROWIE

'Round waterhole.'

BOOKMARK

A slightly odd corruption of 'pukumako', meaning 'flintstone axe'.

BORDERTOWN

Not actually *on* South Australia's border with Victoria, but a pretty lengthy walk to its west, Bordertown was built in 1852 to give miners a place to rest as they travelled to and from the gold fields. The South Australian government had issued instructions that it be built 'as close as possible' to the border – but 19 kilometres was as close as it got.

BREAKNECK HILL

John Parnam may have been great at driving bullocks, but sensitive he was not.

Actually, he wasn't even that great at driving bullocks. It's said that in 1870 or thereabouts, this farmer drove his team to the top of a hill, then stopped to admire the 'magnificent view'. He thus 'did not notice that the bullocks had moved on downhill', with fatal results for one of the 'polers'.

History does not record the poler's name, but thanks to the name that John Parnam gave to the hill, we at least know he broke his neck.

CADELL

Nice guys may finish last, but bad guys can end up dead.

One such bad guy, Captain Francis Cadell, also ended up as the namesake for a town on the Murray. While he was admittedly one of the first men to map it, most of Cadell's career was spent either whaling or in the slave trade. Or in New Zealand, helping to kill off the Maoris.

Considered an 'overrated braggart', he was eventually murdered by one of his crew.

CALTOWIE

'Waterhole belonging to the sleepy lizard.'

CAPE ADIEUX

Australians all, let us rejoice, for we do not speak French.

But mon Dieu, it was a close-run thing. Just 12 years after the English established a colony at Sydney Cove, Napoleon dispatched two ships to explore the continent for the purpose of 'observation and research'. Boasting botanists, zoologists, hydrographers and astronomers, the *Naturaliste* and the *Geographe* spent three years charting our south and west coasts, until at Cape Adieux they at last said 'adieux'.

But did they really mean 'See you later'? Many historians argue that until Napoleon lost his navy at the Battle of Trafalgar in 1805, he had had plans to invade Sydney Cove. It was certainly something recommended by the *Naturaliste*'s 'chief zoologist' in a recently released secret report.

COCKALEECHIE

A choice between haggis and pizza is not really a choice at all. While Italian restaurants can be found all over the world (as can Chinese restaurants, Thai restaurants, Spanish restaurants and so on), you don't see too many Scottish restaurants outside of Scotland or hell.

To illustrate why, I give you Scotland's national soup, cock-a-leekie, a sort of rice porridge with 'boiled cock and leeks'. Strangely enough, it seems to have had at least one Australian fan, because he gave its name (or a variant of it) to a sheep run in South Australia.

COFFIN BAY

Denial. Anger. Bargaining. Depression. Acceptance. People who find themselves stuck in South Australia generally go through all five stages of grief.

But there's no need to contemplate ending it all, just because the state also happens to contain Coffin Bay. A tiny town on the Eyre Peninsula (an area famous for its wheat), Coffin Bay didn't get its name from some suicidal local for whom the thrill of wheat production had started to pall.

No, it just comes from Sir Isaac Coffin – an otherwise insignificant English civil servant who just happened to be friends with Matthew Flinders, the man who 'discovered' the bay.

COONALPYN

'Barren woman.'

CORNY POINT

Shall I start this entry with a corny joke? Oops, seems I already did.

Anyway, moving on. If you can overlook its towns, roads, farms and beaches, Yorke Peninsula, a bit west of Adelaide, kind of more or less looks like a foot.

Corny Point, on its 'sole', kind of juts out a bit, which reminded Matthew Flinders of a callus (or corn).

DEAD MANS PASS

Not long after the establishment of Adelaide, several settlers set out north to see if they could find a place for a country town. Before reaching what's now Gawler, they passed a man who would not be living there – or, indeed, anywhere else.

'We were surprised to find a dead man buried in an upright posture and plastered with clay,' recalled one of the settlers, of the place they named 'Dead Mans Pass'. 'No part of the body was visible except the toes. The wild dogs discovered the corpse, and it had somewhat mangled feet. It was evidently a white man.'

DEVILS GARDENS RESERVE

The devil may be in the detail, but he's in South Australia as well. The state boasts a dangerous road known as Devils Elbow, and a hard-to-climb mountain called Devils Peak.

But Satan seems to have done most of his best work at Devils Gardens Reserve, 90 kilometres north of Adelaide. 'I have vivid memories of several [bullock] teams bogged and almost embedded for some days,' recalled a writer in the 1930s. 'The lurid language, added to the persistent crack of the whip as it re-echoed through the dense mallee, impressed upon my young mind the conviction that the area was aptly named.'

ENCOUNTER BAY

In 1802, England and France had been at war for years – and not just in Europe, but all over the world. They'd fought in America and in Canada, in the Atlantic and the Carribean, and throughout Egypt and the Middle East.

So when England's Matthew Flinders encountered a French ship off the south coast of Australia, he hoisted the flag, loaded the cannons, and dutifully made ready for war. Those on board Le *Geographe*, however, were keen for le truce: they were scientists, not soldiers. The two 'enemy' captains ended up having a nice cup of tea, before sailing on with a 'Bon voyage!'.

FARINA

For every great visionary who had a dream and then achieved it, there is a William Francis Jervois. South Australia's governor in the 1880s, his dream was to create a fertile farmland on the edge of the desert, and so build 'the granary of the north'.

Prompted by an unusually wet wet season, his government accordingly funded several large farms right next to a brand new, and rather large, town. It had hotels, churches, banks and breweries, several blacksmiths, and a state-of-the-art school.

Christened 'Farina', after the Latin word for grain, it is, of course, now a ghost town. Simply dreaming big wasn't enough. To grow crops, you also need rain.

FLINDERS RANGES

What do the following places have in common: the Flinders Ranges, Flinders Chase National Park, Flinders Park, Flinders Bay, Flinders Way, Flinders Street, Flinders Highway and Flinders University.

No idea? Well, I'll tell you: they were all named after Matthew Flinders. The first man to circumnavigate Australia, and confirm that it is indeed a continent, that explorer has had over 100 places named after him – but, sadly, not a single one has been named after his cat.

Black with white feet, and a white star on his chest, Trim was born on the HMS *Reliance*, en route from the Cape of Good Hope, but almost immediately fell overboard. After he 'managed to swim back to the vessel and climb aboard by scaling a rope', Flinders and the crew came to admire his 'strong survival instinct and intelligence' and made him their companion on all of their voyages.

FOUL BAY

It's because of Matthew Flinders that we call Australia 'Australia' – but, having said that, he also came up with 'Foul Bay'.

There's nothing foul about this South Australian beach (though the decaying seaweed can admittedly get a bit whiffy). All in all, it's actually nice. But it's true its shifting sands don't provide a great place to anchor, which was why Flinders was so unimpressed.

GLUEPOT RESERVE

'Low-lying, swampy and saline-affected', this rainy valley just north of Waikerie was a bad place to put a dirt road.

But somebody did it anyway, of course, and over time it proved so boggy its nickname became the 'glue pot'.

GREAT AUSTRALIAN BIGHT

Have you ever wondered what the hell a 'bight' is? Well, I'm told that it simply means 'bay'.

HARVEYS RETURN

To be honest, I haven't researched this, but my hunch is that Kangaroo Island near Adelaide was once home to quite a few kangaroos.

It used to have quite a few seals, as well – plus a few sealers, sadly for them. A Mr Harvey was one of the many men who spent his time shooting and skinning these creatures, but it seems that on one such expedition, he somehow managed to get lost. As days turned into weeks, his fellow sealers assumed he was gone for good, but he eventually returned to a tiny cove we now call Harveys Return.

HOPE VALLEY

It took a lot to discourage William Holden, a nineteenth-century Adelaide butcher who later became a well-known journalist. The suburb of Hope Valley was named during his meat-slicing days, when a fire destroyed either his shop or his home. But 'far from feeling downcast by these misfortunes', Holden felt himself 'inspired by hope'.

HORNY POINT

A jutting-out bit of Thistle Island, Horny Point is shaped a bit like a horn. Let's all cross our fingers and hope that this is how it got its name.

HUMBUG SCRUB

According to *Adelaide Now*, Humbug Scrub was given its curious name because it reminded the surveyor of Barrosa, where a battle was fought during the Crimean War. It was a siege in which Britain's allies promised much but delivered little, and were thus 'a humbug'.

IRON KNOB

No, this town's name did not come from a porn film starring Hung Lo, Lance Bush and Dick Long. It refers to a nearby outcrop of pure iron ore, some of which was used to make the Sydney Harbour Bridge.

LAKE ALEXANDRINA

Not far from Kangaroo Island, this lake was 'discovered' in 1828 and named after Her Royal Highness Princess Alexandrina of Kent, the then heir to the British throne.

A nice gesture, but perhaps a wasted one, as the princess much preferred her middle name. We now call her Queen Victoria.

LAKE EYRE

'An eye for an eye and a tooth for a tooth,' says someone in the Bible. Edward Eyre, on the other hand, would have extracted about a thousand eyes if anyone ever dared to take one of his own.

The man who 'discovered' Lake Eyre, and modestly lent his name to it, should really be remembered for his time as governor of Jamaica, which ended up in a murder trial. Controversially acquitted, Eyre had reacted to a riot from a handful of locals by sending the troops in with orders to kill. Despite meeting no organised resistance whatsoever, they shot dead 439 men, women and children.

Governor Eyre then arrested and executed a further 169 'rioters', flogged a further 600 people and burnt down about 1000 homes.

LAKE MASSACRE

As massacres go, the one at Lake Massacre would not make much of a horror film. For one thing, there was only one victim. And for another, he died of dysentery.

The lake was so named by a party sent into the desert to find out what had happened to Burke and Wills. After discovering the body of one of Burke's companions in a grave right by the lake, they concluded the whole lot of them must have been massacred, and quickly turned around and headed for home.

LONG SLEEP PLAIN

If you're one of those people who loves history, a place like, say, Paris is a feast for the eyes. You can go to Place de la Bastille, where the Bastille was stormed, or Montmartre, where Saint Denis was martyred. The Arc de Triomphe commemorates some of Napoleon's great triumphs; the Avenue Victor-Hugo, that great author's life.

To be fair, South Australia also tries to celebrate important historical events. But perhaps it needs to try harder. Take Long Sleep Plain, for example. This stretch of land between Port Augusta and Whyalla is said to commemorate 'a wagon driver who fell asleep on a journey between these two places'.

Lest we forget . . .

LOOS

'War! Huh! Yeah! What is it good for?' sang someone-or-other in the 1960s, most likely while wearing flares.

But the answer, I am glad to report, is *not* in fact 'absolutely nothing'. World War I did a little bit to improve the atlas, insofar as it forced the right-thinking residents of Buchfelde to ditch their suburb's Germanic name. For a replacement, they chose to honour a small French town on the Western Front that had just been the scene of a major conflict.

But it had probably also been the scene of a few cheap jokes. That town's name was Loos.

MAMUNGKUKUMPURANGKUNTJUNYA HILL

'Where the devil urinates.'

MARALINGA

Prepared to hear something amazing?

Well, prepare again: this is 'quite interesting' at best. The remote western area home to the Pitjantjatjara people until the British blew up nuclear bombs there – got its new name from a word meaning 'field of thunder'. Thunder, of course, is loud and destructive, much like a nuclear bomb.

Woomera's name is also non-coincidental. After the RAF chose it as a site to test the efficacy of its missiles, they named it after the local word for spear.

MEMORY COVE

You don't need a history book to know that Matthew Flinders had a few difficult days as he sailed past South Australia. You just need to look at a map. The state boasts an Anxious Bay and a Cape Catastrophe, a Thorny Passage and a Dangerous Reef.

Most poignant, perhaps, is Memory Cove: a place he named in memory of the eight men he dispatched one evening in a dinghy to find water onshore. As darkness fell, the waves picked up – and the little boat failed to return. The crew found a few planks on the beach the next day, but never found any trace of the men.

Their names live on in the surrounding islands (Thistle, Taylor, Smith, Lewis, Grindal, Little, Hopkins and Williams) and in a story Flinders liked to recall. 'It concerned Mr Thistle, and later other crewmen, who visited a fortune teller before the ship left Portsmouth. Thistle was told he would be lost at sea. The crew were also told sailors would be lost, but not in the ship they left the harbour in. The prophecies proved to be tragically accurate.'

MILANG

'A place of sorcery.'

MOUNT BABBAGE

Christopher Columbus, Marco Polo, Ferdinand Magellan, Captain Cook.

So might begin a list of history's great explorers – but even at the bottom, you won't see the name Benjamin Babbage. The 'discoverer' of Mount Babbage didn't discover all that much else in 1856, when he was sent by the South Australian government to look for gold. 'By the end of six months his explorations had scarcely penetrated beyond the limits of pastoral settlement.'

'Impatient at his slow rate of progress', the government ordered him back.

MOUNT COMPASS

A few things happened in 1840 that probably fall into the category of 'Historical Event'. The British stopped sending convicts to New South Wales, for example, and laid claim to the land of New Zealand. Napoleon died, postage stamps were born, and Samuel Morse patented the telegraph. Antarctica was discovered to be a continent, and construction of the Palace of Westminster began.

And who could forget what happened in South Australia? On a small hill south of Willunga, as you know, Governor Gawler mislaid his compass. It was this event that settlers naturally chose to commemorate when they moved to 'Mount Compass' later that year.

MOUNT GAMBIER

Courage does not consist in the absence of fear but in the ability to overcome it. A brave person is someone who's scared of something, but shrugs their shoulders and carries on.

James Gambier, the naval commander who gave his name to Mount Gambier, may well have felt a little scared a few years later, at 1809's Battle of the Basque Roads. When he saw the pride of Napoleon's fleet floating before him, cannons loaded, he would surely have needed to overcome fear.

Unfortunately, though, he didn't. Though 'Dismal Jimmy' was later acquitted in a court martial, his career never recovered from accusations of cowardice after he failed to send his section of the fleet into the fray. 'I never saw a man so unfit for the command as Your Lordship,' one of his fellow admirals is said to have screamed.

MOUNT HOPELESS

If at first you don't succeed, try, try again. But if, after all that, you *still* haven't succeeded, it's probably time to give up.

Such seemed to be Edward Eyre's thinking after his third, and furthest, journey into South Australia's north finally ended at the top of Mount Hopeless. 'Cheerless and hopeless indeed was the prospect before us,' he wrote of the 'desolate and forbidding' view. The search for fertile farmland was over, he decided: South Australia was dry desert through and through.

MOUNT HORROCKS

There are lots of ways to die in this world – and they include being shot by a camel.

Such was the fate which befell John Ainsworth Horrocks, the man who 'discovered' Mount Horrocks. A few weeks into his first and last expedition through the Flinders Ranges, this explorer was sitting on his camel, loading his gun in order to go shoot some lunch. But the camel suddenly lurched for no reason, knocking Horrocks forward and causing the gun to go off in his mouth.

Less than a month later, he was dead from gangrene – and I'm sorry to say that he didn't die graciously. The camel was 'executed on his express wish' without even so much as a trial.

MYPONGA

Don't worry: there'll be no jokes here about Yourponga, let alone Hisponga or Herponga or Theirponga. My job is to report the facts, and these are that Myponga, 60 kilometres south of Adelaide, is an Indigenous word that means 'cliffs'.

NACKARA

A farming town east of Peterborough, Nackara may be named after the Indigenous word for 'black duck' – black duck being one of the 20-odd foods boys were forbidden from eating, lest they grow up ugly or feminine. Pink-eyed ducks were also forbidden, along with black-and-white geese.

NOTT WELL

I would give you a better pun about Mr William Nott's water-hole but unfortunately I am not well.

NULLABOR PLAIN

Nullabor's name is a bit of an overstatement, as it *does* have a handful of trees.

Did that sentence make sense? It will after you read this one: 'nullus arbor' is Latin for 'no trees'.

OB FLAT

Branding cows is a painful business involving hot irons, burnt skin and loud shrieks. So we can be grateful, I guess, that Mr O Beswick chose to only brand his cattle with his initials, 'OB', rather than spell out his whole name.

OB cows became such a common sight in the area that it eventually became OB Flat.

OCHRE COVE

No place for a children's birthday party, Ochre Cove is said to have got its blood-red colour from actual blood. Various ancestral beings have been attacked there in Indigenous folklore, and it seems that not all of them fought back well.

OODNADATTA

'Smelly water.'

ORROROO

I don't quite know what 'Orroroo' means, but I do know a good joke when I hear one. It's said that when South Australia's postmaster received a request to establish a post office in the town, he replied, 'Dear me! There are only two letters in Orroroo. What do you want a post office for?'

PARIS CREEK

Property buyers beware: this name is a touch misleading. A nice enough place in the Adelaide Hills, so long as you like grass and cows, Paris Creek was named after an early settler called Robert Paris.

PINKY FLAT

Some people like red wine, while others prefer white. And then we have those who drink 'pinky'.

Pinky Flat received its name during the Depression, when it was used as a sort of campground for the unemployed. Many of them, it's said, were driven to drown their sorrows with pinky: a 'young, immature wine, with sugar or syrup added to sweeten, and enough raw spirit thrown in to prevent fermentation'.

POLLYS WELL

While you can no longer get water from Polly's Well, it's still a major landmark (well, okay, the only landmark) in the tiny town of Peake.

It may be a good thing that it's now bricked up, because the well's water mightn't have tasted so great. Some say Polly was a horse who used to draw water from the 18-metre deep well . . . until somehow she managed to fall in.

POOCHERA

While it does, indeed, have an underground sewer, the town of Poochera on the Eyre Peninsula is in no way named after poo. The name is said to come from King Poojeri, an Indigenous resident of years ago.

PORT WAKEFIELD

Unlike Sydney and Brisbane and Hobart and Perth, Adelaide was never a penal colony: right from the start, it was convict-free.

The city owes its comparatively upmarket origins to an economist called Edward Wakefield. In 1829's *Sketch of a Proposal for Colonizing Australasia*, he argued that Australia would be well-served by a system of 'concentrated free settlement' – essentially, setting aside land for a new city, selling plots at high prices, and using the profits to entice immigrant workers. Relying on convict labour wasn't just unedifying, Wakefield wrote, it was also uneconomical.

Assorted politicians eventually agreed, and invited the Londoner to draft 1834's *South Australia Act* – legislation which quickly led to the creation of Adelaide.

All of which makes it somewhat ironic that Wakefield wrote his book from Newgate Gaol. He was serving three years for kidnap at the time, after abducting a 15-year-old heiress.

PRINCES HIGHWAY

One of South Australia's more useful roads (insofar as it leads straight to Melbourne), the Princes Highway got its name from one of England's more useless kings. The Prince of Wales in 1920, when he visited the colonies to cut a few ribbons, Edward Windsor became king in 1936, only to abdicate later that year.

His reason, of course, was that he wanted to marry a divorcee, and this was something that a reigning monarch just couldn't do. But many historians insist that Edward would have been happy to hop back on the throne as a Nazi puppet, had the Germans won World War II. Whether or not that's true, he was certainly an ardent admirer of the regime, who enjoyed dinner with Goebbels, tea with Göring and a private meeting with Hitler himself. 'The Germans and the British races are one. They should always be one,' he once said, to the moustached one's approval.

ROGUES GULLY

It's tempting to always think well of whalers, with their six-foot-long lethal harpoons and adorable little knives for blubber-stripping. But one must maintain an open mind.

Alfred Weaver was well aware of this, so when four 'half-famished', 'suspicious-looking' whalers turned up at his cattle station looking for work, he took the precaution of telling a policeman the next time he went into town.

And it was a good thing he did. 'The noted police officer pricked up his ears,' *The Chronicle* reported years later, and 'told Weaver that he had just received information that four desperate criminals of the bushranging type had escaped from Tasmania and . . . were wanted for murder [having] . . . cold-bloodedly blown out the brains of a police inspector.'

The story continued: 'I have not the space here to give you the full story of their apprehension, beyond saying that the police surprised and arrested them while they were cooking their evening meal and that [the policeman] carried to his grave the marks of the struggle which took place.'

Had they not been captured, the four rogues later confessed, their plan had been to 'seize a ship, murder the officers and such of the crew as were deemed hostile, and then to make for Western Australia'. But instead, they 'were returned to Hobart under strong escort and there paid the penalty of their crimes on the scaffold'.

ROTTEN BAY

There may have been something rotten in the state of Denmark, but everything seems just fine in Rotten Bay. It's a perfectly pleasant part of Boston Island, with plenty of sun, sand and surf.

So why the name? One theory is that it's a rotten place to anchor, because of all the razor fish which live in the water and like to slash away at the rope. But it seems a little unlikely that razor fish could actually do this. Not least because there aren't many there.

ROYAL PARK

Royal Park isn't a particularly great name, but it could certainly be a lot worse. Actually, it *has* been a lot worse. During Adelaide's early years this western suburb was known as 'Piggery Park', due to the smell from a nearby abattoir.

And it's not the only South Australian place name to have some extreme plastic surgery over the years. Another suburb, Paradise, began life as 'Shepley', while Chapel Valley was 'Cobbledick Swamp'. Cape Banks started out as 'Gloomy Cape', while Chiton Rocks could probably be considered an improvement on that area's Indigenous name: 'Jingeinju,' meaning 'pubic hair'.

SANDY BAGOTS POOL

Some place names improve over time. Others definitely don't.

This tiny waterhole got its name from a medieval saint who was murdered in cold blood in his church. And I'm sorry to say that St a'Beckett continued to suffer in heaven as he saw the name of 'Saint a'Beckett's Pool' slowly morph into 'Sandy Bagots'.

SECRET ROCK

Famous for sinking a steamship way back in 1887, Secret Rock is not so secret now.

SEVENHILL

This Clare Valley town was named by a Catholic priest after the Seven Hills of Ancient Rome.

Though, technically speaking, they're more like *three* hills, plus a volcanic ridge with four smallish bumps.

SHAG COVE

Lots of shags here, my friend. 'Shags', of course, being birds.

SNOWTOWN

There's no snow in Snowtown, just a few houses and roads and shops and pubs, and, of course, a few body-filled barrels. The town name comes from a Thomas Snow, the assistant of a former South Australia governor.

SULTANA POINT

No sultanas are sold on this remote rural headland, but you might see a *Sultana* if you went for a swim. The name comes from a ship which was wrecked a mile or so from the coast.

TUNGKILLO

'Witchetty grub.'

VERDUN

The Royal Family, as you might know, were not always the Windsors, but adopted the name during World War I. Properly speaking, their surname is 'Saxe-Coburg-Gotha', but PR-wise this wasn't what you might call helpful when the whole of England was fighting the Hun.

Their German-sounding subjects had similar problems. Friedrichs were rechristened Fredericks all over the Empire, while Johanns became Josephs and Johns.

But the biggest change came in a German-sounding state. No less than 69 South Australian towns were cleansed of their 'German-ness' during the Great War, so as to become all patriotic and pure. Among them: Cape Wondoma (Cape Bauer), Panpandie Rock (Berlin Rock), Bethany (Bethanien), Weeroopa (Bismarck), Birdwood (Blumberg), Lakkari (Blumenthal), Loos (Buchfelde), Kunden (Carlsruhe), Mount Yerila (Ehrenbreitstein), Ernaballa Creek (Ferdinand Creek), Mount Warrabillinna (Mount Ferdinand), Tangari (Friedrichstadt), Tarnma (Friedrichswalde), Polygon Ridge (Gebhardt's Hills), Benara

Creek (German Creek), Tappa Pass (German Pass), Vimy Ridge (Germantown Hill), Parnggi Well (Gottlieb's Well), Karalta (Grunberg), Verdun (Grunthal), Ambleside (Hahndorf – reinstated in 1935), Larelar Mound (Hasse's Mound), Kobandilla (Heidelberg), Marree (Hergott Springs), Punthari (Hildesheim), Karawirra (Hoffnungsthal), Kerkanya (Jaenschtown), Mount Kitchener (Kaiserstuhl), Kilto (Klaebes), Gaza (Klemzig), Marti Rock (Krause Rock), Beatty (Krichauff), Kabminye (Kronsdorf), Kaldukee (Langdorf), Bilyara (Langmeil), Tweedvale (Lobethal), Mount Kauto (Mount Meyer), Yandina Hill (Muller's Hill), Mamburdi (Neudorf), Dimchurch (Neukirch), Willyaroo (New Hamburg), Gomersal (New Mecklenburg), Olivedale (Oliventhal), Peterborough (Petersburg), Mons (Rhine Hill), Kongolia (Rhine Park), Cambrai (Rhine Villa), Rosedale (Rosenthal), Boongala (Schoenthal), Warre (Schreiberhau), Dorrien (Seppelts), Bultawilta (Siegersdorf), Stonefield (Steinfeld), Summerfield (Summerfeldt), Teerkoore (Vogelsang's Corner), Karun Nob (Wusser's Nob).

About the only German place name that *wasn't* changed was Adelaide – a city named after a German princess.

VICTOR HARBOR

Notice anything odd about the spelling here? That's right: there's no 'u' in Harbor. Just like Outer Harbor, 100 kilometres north, the town of Victor Harbor has always been spelled the American way, and nobody quite knows why.

WALLAROO

'Wallaby's urine.'

YANKALILLA

Mourning a loved one is a difficult business, and it's even harder if the corpse misbehaves. According to a Professor Tindale, the town of Yankalilla comes from a word meaning 'falling' and refers to a Dreamtime myth. A man's 'sister's mummified body began to fall into pieces here, as he was carrying it to Cape Jervis for burial'.

YUNTA

'Vagina.'

Northern Territory

For a while there, the Northern Territory could have been 'Kingsland', though 'Centralia' and 'Territoria' were options as well. A part of South Australia until it was carved off in 1911 and put under Commonwealth control, the Top End has also been known as Alexandrina Land in its time, after the name that Queen Victoria went by as princess, while Macassan traders from Sulawesi supposedly called it something along the lines of 'Marage'.

Mostly, however, it has been known to outsiders as 'that hot remote place that we don't want to live in'. The Macassans never set up permanent camps, and the Dutch ships that sailed by in the 1600s quickly sailed off again, though they did leave behind names like Groote Eylandt ('Big Island'), the Gulf of Carpentaria and Arnhem Land.

In 1803 Matthew Flinders came by, naming places like Melville Bay, Mount Saunders, Point Dundas and Drimmie

Head, followed a decade or two later by Captain Phillip Parker King (Melville Island, Bathurst Island: both bigwigs back home).

During the 1820s the British established a series of forts, and abandoned them all just as quickly. And that was essentially where matters lay until 5 February 1869, when South Australia's government established a settlement at Port Darwin (only to wash their hands of it 42 years later).

The upshot off all this hands-offishness is that the Northern Territory still has a healthy sampling of Indigenous place names. If only we could work out what the hell they all mean.

ALICE SPRINGS

On either side of the Todd River you'll find the city of Alice Springs.

Both the river and the city got their name from a Lady Alice Todd, a woman who never went near either of them, or (as far as we know) did a great deal much else. Born in Cambridge in 1826, she met 22-year-old Charles Todd when she was, um, 12, and married him six years later. Charles, being some kind of science whiz, was dispatched to Australia to take charge of a telegraph line that was being laid through the desert. Lady Alice came with him, of course, but only as far as Adelaide. She never got close to the little town that sprang up around her husband's telegraph station.

'The story of Sir Charles and Lady Alice Todd is basically the story of all the early pioneers,' wrote a thoroughly modern-sounding historian in the '50s. 'It is the story of a great man fulfilling his destiny in a new land, encouraged by the tenderness, wisdom and gentle dignity of an English bride.'

ALLIGATOR RIVER

No alligators in this river, so swimmers need not fear them. But they should probably keep an eye out for crocodiles.

ARNHEM

While it's become synonymous with Indigenous history and culture, the name 'Arnhem Land' is actually Dutch. It was bestowed on the top right bit of the Northern Territory by the crew of the *Arnhem*, a seventeenth-century ship, which was in turn named after an old Dutch town.

BEES CREEK

No bees here, I'm pleased to say. Just Tom Bee, a surveyor's assistant.

BERRIMAH

Darwin is not always the first place in Australia that foreigners visit, but things were very different during World War II. Conscious that the Japanese might come and bomb the city (as, indeed, they eventually did), the army built a number of new military depots, around which new suburbs later sprang.

One of these suburbs was in the east of the city, and was thus named 'Berrimah' by army head honchos, that being a local phrase meaning 'in the east'.

Consultation with locals clearly wasn't their thing. It actually means 'to the south'.

Darwin

These days, of course, we know a lot about Charles Darwin: big beard, big theory, big brain, big deal.

But in 1839, when a sailor named John Stokes gave his name to a small cove in the Northern Territory, that groundbreaking biologist wasn't a celebrity at all. The father of evolution didn't actually publish his theory until 1859. Until then, he was just an obscure bird fancier who'd spent part of his youth on a trip around the world.

But that one long voyage, as it happens, had been on the *Beagle* – the very same ship that Stokes was on a few years later when he saw a potential place for a port. Not thinking much of the find, he named it Port Darwin in tribute to his friend, never imagining that it would become a major city. The name was simply 'an appropriate opportunity of convincing an old shipmate and friend that he still lived in our memory'.

But how appropriate was it, really? Charles had, in fact, visited Australia on said round-the-world voyage – and it doesn't seem like he was overly impressed.

'Farewell Australia,' he wrote in his diary as the *Beagle* left our shores for the last time. 'You are a rising infant and doubtless some day will reign a great princess in the South. But you are too great and ambitious for affection, yet not great enough for respect. I leave your shores without sorrow or regret.'

Ok, then . . .

Berry Springs *Edwin S Berry, part of the South Australia survey group*

Casuarina Square *A species of tree*

Cullen Bay *A local solicitor from the 1870s*

Holmes Jungle Nature Park *Named after Felix Holmes, who 'owned a butchery, ice works, cordial factory and power station and ran cattle in the Jungle' during the 1930s*

Knuckey Street *Richard Randall Knuckey, a surveyor*

Lake Alexander *Alec Fong Lim, Lord Mayor of Darwin, 1984–90*

Leanyer Recreation Park *Nobody knows*

Marrara Oval *Nobody knows*

Mindil Beach *'Sweet nut'*

Mitchell Street *AJ Mitchell, surveyor*

Parap Markets *From Paraparap, a Victorian property owned by an early Darwin administrator*

Smith Street *AH Smith, surveyor*

Tiger Brennan Drive *Harold 'Tiger' Brennan, Mayor of Darwin, 1972–75*

FANNIE BAY

This Darwin suburb is thought to be named after an opera singer who performed for South Australia's chief surveyor a few weeks before he left to found Darwin.

A problem with this theory is that her name was *Fanny* Carandini, but it's not really such a big one when you consider just how much of the Northern Territory is badly spelled. The Katherine River, for example, was named after *Catherine* Chambers, while Frazer Hill was named after Dawn *Fraser*, and Tylers Pass after David *Theile*.

GOVE PENINSULA

Once home to the Royal Australian Air Force, and now mostly known for Gove Airport, the Gove Peninsula was rather appropriately named after a pilot.

A pilot who, rather less appropriately, died in a midair collision.

GUNBARREL HIGHWAY

An isolated desert track that stretches from the Northern Territory to Western Australia via South Australia, the Gunbarrel Highway is not in fact 'as straight as a gun barrel', as the name might suggest.

Quite curvy in places, and very curvy everywhere else, it got its name from the company that built it: Gunbarrel Road Constructions.

HONEYMOON GAP

Essentially meaning 'sweet month', the word 'honeymoon' is thought to refer to the idea that the first month of marriage is the sweetest.

If that were true, then Bob and Vicki Darken could well have been in trouble. After they married in Darwin in 1942, the couple ventured out to what was then 'Temple Gap', an isolated little waterhole 17 kilometres away.

And they both had a lovely time there. Apart from the fact that their car broke down and it rained every single moment of every single day.

HUMPTY DOO

No-one quite knows where the name Humpty Doo came from (though I assume we all agree it's great). The best guess is that it's a corruption of 'umdidu' ('resting place'), though it could also come from a ye olde colloquialism that basically meant 'cock-up'.

If the town's name *does* actually refer to a cock-up, Nostradamus must somehow have been involved, for the town's main claim to fame came 50 years *after* it was named. At that time it became the centre of a grand-scale experiment that involved irrigating 303 000 hectares with the aim of growing vast swathes of tropical crops. The Northern Territory's future, said cabinet ministers, scientists and international investors, lay in becoming the food bowl of Asia.

Only, of course, it didn't. 'Everything that could go wrong did go wrong,' says the *Sydney Morning Herald* of the cock-up.

'Wild buffaloes moved in and started destroying the paddies and eating the crops. Rats appeared and wrought havoc. The birds consumed the seeds as quickly as the company could plant them. The soil proved to be too saline and the drainage was inadequate.'

Within four years, the would-be paddy fields were abandoned. 'It was one of the great failed agricultural experiments.'

LASSETER HIGHWAY

Land values in central Melbourne are idiotically high, and if you want to live near the Sydney coast, sell a kidney cos they're higher still. But it may be that Australia's most valuable land is 1500 kilometres away from the coast, and almost as far from a funky bar. According to Harold Lasseter, the man after whom Lasseter Highway was named, there's a shimmering, six-mile-long reef of gold somewhere south-west of Alice Springs. He stumbled across it in 1907, while out prospecting for rubies, but could never quite retrace his steps.

That, at least, was what Lasseter told a group of investors some three decades later – and, weirdly enough, many seemed to believe him. He used their money to mount the best-equipped gold-seeking expedition in Australia's history. And he used that expedition to get lost and die.

MACDONNELL RANGES

Much like Lady Alice of Alice Springs, South Australian governor Richard MacDonnell never saw the mountain range that now bears his name. One of those professional colonial administrator types (he also governed Hong Kong, Nova Scotia, Gambia and the West Indies in the course of a medal-strewn career), he was too busy discouraging charity back in Adelaide, because he believed it 'fostered pauperism and sloth'.

MARRAKAI

According to a letter to the editor in a 1971 edition of *Walkabout*, this name came about when 'the earliest white mapmakers asked a group of Aborigines for the native name of the area ... The natives, knowing that the white man's name for a nearby river had been "Mary", and aiming to please, tried to say it was "the Mary River" area. It all came out as "Mary-kai" (the word "kai" being that of a river)' – hence the name Marrakai.

OLGAS

Being married to a king who shared his bed with three American men, Queen Olga of Württemberg didn't have any children, or all that much in the way of companionship.

To help pass the hours she took up natural science, collecting minerals, corresponding with intellectuals and taking a keen interest in newly discovered plants. She was thus in a good position to appreciate the good work of Ferdinand von Mueller, a German-born botanist who went to Australia in 1847 and helped discover, name and found this and that.

To show her appreciation, Olga made him a baron. And then Ferdinand appreciated her right back.

PALMERSTON

Twice England's prime minister, and a long-time foreign secretary, Lord Palmerston wasn't *always* starting wars, as his reputation suggests, but that wasn't from a lack of trying. Convinced that his country was 'the champion of justice and right', the man after whom the city of Palmerston was named never passed up an opportunity to annoy another country or, better still, send in the troops.

'If I were not a Frenchman, I should wish to be an Englishman,' a powerful Frenchman, wishing to be friendly, once said. 'If I were not an Englishman, I should wish to be an Englishman,' the warmonger coolly replied.

RUM JUNGLE

No-one can quite agree why Rum Jungle is 'Rum Jungle', but the general consensus is that the story involves rum.

My favourite version comes from Bill Beatty. He says that some miners once 'arrived in this district carrying a load of 750 ounces of gold. On the uninviting spot they met a teamster who boasted of his rum cargo. Gathering round, the miners partook of the teamster's hospitality to such good effect that they knew no more for some hours. Consciousness came, and with it the discovery that the gold, their horses, and the team-ster had vanished. Every man in the district began a search which lasted for months until the thieving teamster and the gold were found. Then, once again, Rum Jungle lived up to its name.'

SIMPSON DESERT

The world's largest sand dune desert – 70 000 square miles of bright white and burnt orange, and salt lakes, sand, swamps and scrubs – is named after a maker of washing machines. A former president of the South Australian branch of the Royal Geographical Society, Alfred Simpson never actually went near the Simpson Desert, but he gave lots of money to explorers who did.

TORRES STRAIT

The Torres Strait should have been the *Quierós* Strait, only a mutiny got in the way.

The waterway that separates Australia from New Guinea was first mapped by one Luís Vaz de Torres, the captain of the second of three Spanish ships that had been sent to explore the Pacific. The *first* ship to sail, captained by the expedition's commander Pedro de Quierós, should by rights have been the first one to reach it, but his sailors mutinied and made him turn around.

ULURU

Now known by a proper noun which means 'Uluru' and nothing else, Australia's most beautiful landmark is also its most sacred for many citizens. Tourists are asked not to climb up Uluru, and any sort of development is naturally banned.

So all in all, it seems like a good thing that it's no longer called Ayers Rock. Sir Henry Ayers was, after all, a politician who made his money out of building mines.

YELLOW WATER

No, there's no pee in this billabong (or at least no more than the usual amount). But it can apparently look a bit yellow at times, thanks to the way it reflects the setting sun.

Australian Capital Territory

A compromise, as someone once put it, is a process by which two parties get together and agree to do something that neither of them really wants. In the lead up to Federation in 1901, Australia's two main cities entered into just such a process, because they both wanted to be the new nation's capital.

The result, of course, was that neither is. It was decided that Melbourne would host the government on a temporary basis while a new capital was built somewhere near Sydney. Just *where* exactly was a question which took years to answer, with locations like Albury, Wagga Wagga and Dalgety all very seriously considered.

In 1908, parliament finally chose a site in the foothills of the Australian Alps: a 'treeless and sparsely settled plain' that was mostly inhabited by mosquitoes and sheep. The main appeal seems to have been that it was surrounded by rivers, and boasted the sort of cool climate that creates a 'hardier race'.

But what to call it? Well, the 'Australian Capital Territory' was straightforward enough, but the name of the proposed capital city was more problematic. Home to the Ngunnawal people for perhaps 20000 years, along with a handful of sheep farmers since 1824, the site had up until that point been known by a variety of names, including 'Nganbra', 'Pialligo', 'Kambera' and 'Kgamberry'. In recent decades, the names had slowly merged into 'Canberry', though 'Canberra' was becoming more popular.

So Canberra, then? Well, while it was a good name, it wasn't necessarily a great one – particularly given the very real possibility that it means 'cleavage'. In 1912, therefore, the Department of Home Affairs invited citizens to come up with some alternatives – and 764 suggestions were promptly sent in. The most popular seems to have been Austral City, while Federalia was another early frontrunner.

Rather less popular, thanks to a merciful God, were suggestions like Australamooloo, Wheatwoolgold, Federalbus, Quickbarton and Kangaremu, while Sydmeladperbrisho (an amalgamation of all six capital cities) thankfully got short shrift. Other bad ideas included Climax, Back Spur, Eucalypta, Eros, Thirstyville, Cookabura, Empire City, Democratia, Utopia, Cooee, Swindleville, Gonebroke, Olympus, Paradise, Captain Cook and Revenuelia.

When it came to influential people, Prime Minister Andrew Fisher seemed to have liked Myola, for whatever strange reason, while one of his predecessors pushed for Pacifica, and the Minister for Home Affairs wanted Shakespeare.

In the end, the city was officially given its name by the Governor-General's wife, Lady Denman, in a grand(ish) ceremony on Capital Hill. At least 5000 people came along to clap and cheer, along with brass bands, flags and bunting.

It's said that there had been much disagreement in the cabinet as to how the new name should be pronounced: *Can*-berra or Can-*berra*? Since neither word was authentic Ngunnawal, and there was thus no right or wrong, it was decided that whatever pronunciation Lady Denman happened to come up with would, from that moment, be the right one. Amid a fanfare of trumpets, she made her way to the dais, extracted a card from a gold case, glanced at it, paused, paused a bit longer . . . and laid stress upon the first syllable.

When it comes to naming places *within* Canberra, the government's approach has been a touch more scientific. Ever since a submission to parliament in 1927, the vast majority of suburbs have been named after significant Australians. Scientists (Florey), doctors (Flynn) and war heroes (Dunlop) all feature somewhere on the map, along with judges like Latham, Higgins and Evatt.

Canberra being Canberra, no less than 16 suburbs are named after prime ministers, Francis Forde among them, even though he was only prime minister for seven days, though they're yet to find room for Robert Menzies (18 years).

The street names, too, are chosen with care: every single suburb has its own theme. In Banks, for example – a suburb named after Sir Joseph – every street honours a botanist or naturalist; while in Farrar (a suburb named after a farmer), all roads are named after pastoralists.

But where do you find something 'weird and wonderful'? Just try reading on.

BANKS

Sir Joseph Banks was a man worth commemorating – and when it comes to place names, we've done just that. The Canberra suburb of Banks is just one of many bits of Australia that go by his rather bland name.

But it's worth noting that the botanist himself was not bland at all. While he's now best known for collecting plants aboard the *Endeavour*, he also liked to collect women. Fond of going on holidays with 'two or three ladies of pleasure', Banks used the greatest holiday of all – Captain Cook's voyage – as an opportunity to get to know the Queen of Tahiti. It's said that his trousers were stolen while he was inside her tent. Though it was also said that he didn't much need them.

And while Sir Joseph eventually decided to stay home rather than go on Cook's second trip south, the same can't be said for one of his mistresses. Apparently unaware of his last-minute change of plans, one of Banks's acquaintances, a Mr Burnett, did his best to hop aboard in Portugal. Or possibly *her* best. 'Every part of Mr Burnett's behaviour and every action tended to prove that he was a Woman,' Captain Cook later wrote.

BARTON

As we all know (or at least pretend that we do), Australia became an independent country on 1 January 1901, when the six colonies federated, and instead became states.

But becoming a *democratic* country took a bit longer. As a federated nation, it was thought, we needed a federal government straightaway. An actual federal election could wait until March.

So in mid-December 1900, the governor-general to be – a 40-year-old foreigner called Lord Hopetoun – arrived in Australia for the very first time, and thought, *Hmm, whom shall I make prime minister?* Strongly advised to appoint Edmund Barton, a popular leader in the federalist movement, he naturally went with William Lyme. A man who was not only despised by his colleagues, but who had actively opposed Federation, Lyme spent a week asking prospective MPs to form part of his cabinet – and getting told 'no' every time.

On Christmas Day, he finally gave up and suggested Hopetoun try somebody else. His Lordship's second choice, Barton, had no trouble forming a government, or indeed winning an actual election the following March.

COOK

You'd think this suburb would be named after Captain Cook and, while you're not wrong, you're also not right. I'm told that it is *also* named after Sir Joseph Cook, a unionist-turned-free-trader who was prime minister for a Rudd-like 16 months.

Canberra

You might say that Canberra is full of boobs and, technically speaking, you might be correct. While no-one's quite sure what the Ngunnawal word 'Kambera' once meant, as that language is now extinct, the initial thought was that it meant 'meeting place'. Indigenous groups would gather there to work out their differences, went the theory, just as political groups try to today.

But according to a now-dead Ngunnawal elder named Don Bell, the real meaning is much more amusing. Being a flat plain nestled between two round hills (Mount Ainslie and Black Mountain), Canberra, the word, essentially means cleavage: it's the hollow between a woman's breasts.

Aspen Island *Aspen trees*
Brindabella Range *'Two kangaroo rats'*

Gungahlin Drive 'White man's house'

Lake Ginninderra 'Sparkling'

Lake Tuggeranong 'Cold plain'

Mount Majura Named after a place in India its 'discoverer' had visited

Mount Stromlo Nobody knows . . .

Mulligans Flat From 'a man named Mulligan' who once had a hut there

Parkes Way Sir Henry Parkes, six-time premier of colonial New South Wales

Scrivener Dam Charles Scrivener, surveyor

Tidbinbilla Nature Reserve 'A place where boys become men'

Vernon Circle Walter Liberty Vernon, an architect

Wentworth Avenue William Wentworth, explorer

Weston Park Charles Weston, horticulturalist responsible for the forestation of Canberra

'Dual naming', as this dubious practice is known, may soon come to Fraser as well. That Canberra suburb is currently named after a Jim Fraser, a former MP. Reverse those letters and you get a former PM, but if Malcolm Fraser is ever to be honoured with a suburb, it'll be an honour he'll just have to share.

But that still puts Malcolm in a better position than two other former prime ministers: Bob Hawke and John Gorton will probably never get suburbs at all. Canberra, you see, already had a *Hawker* and a *Gordon*: two names that are different, but just not different enough.

According to the ACT Government's Place Names Committee, 'When you have two suburbs with very similar names the issue becomes primarily one of safety, as one of our primary responsibilities is to avoid confusion for emergency services,' says a spokeswoman for the planning authority.

COTTER RIVER

Long before it came into existence, and became the capital of an independent Australia, Canberra had a Cotter River. And it's since built a Cotter Avenue and a Cotter Dam in the Cotter Valley.

You'd suspect that independence from Britain was something Cotter himself would have enjoyed. An Irish rebel turned ACT stockman, he came here a convict in chains after opening fire on His Majesty's troops.

DEAKIN

It is right to remember Alfred Deakin as a great colonial statesman and three-time prime minister. But, let's face it, it's not that much fun.

So let's all focus on the little-known fact that, behind closed doors, he was a major kook. Fond of 'communication with unseen intelligences', Deakin was a regular attendee at seances and a long-serving president of the Association of Spiritualists. He occasionally chatted with the likes of Sophocles, Edmund Burke, JS Mill and John Bunyan – four men who were long since dead.

DUNTROON

Now home to Australia's Royal Military College, Duntroon is really 'Duntrune'. The suburb was named by its original owner after Duntrune Castle, his family's Scottish estate.

But perhaps he was being a bit rash? Duntrune Castle, you see, has long had problems with ghosts: it is haunted by the spirit of an ancient Scottish bagpiper – a man whose hands were cut off by the castle's then residents, and who carries a grudge to this day.

And now the Royal Military College is having ghost problems too. Some time in the '70s, says the *Canberra Times*, soldiers 'started to report glimpses of a glowing ghost of a young woman in 19th-century period costume. Soon after, some residents also complained that a bed, freshly made in the morning, would be found as if it had been slept in later in the day, with pillows hurled around the room'.

FAIRBAIRN

Now home to Canberra's airport, this suburb is named after a former federal Minister for Air and Civil Aviation.

Who, um, died in a plane crash.

GILMORE

Gilmore is not just a Canberra suburb, it's also the name of a national electorate.

This is perhaps odd when you consider that Mary Gilmore, the socialist poet commemorated by both places, did not think much of this nation at all. She ditched our democracy in the 1890s in order to live in 'New Australia', a South American commune.

GREENWAY

One of Australia's most distinguished architects, whose works include Sydney's Government House, Frances Greenway was actually one of *England*'s most distinguished architects until he became a convict after forging a cheque.

Still commemorated in the Canberra suburb, one of Greenway's other honours, somewhat oddly, was being a long-time face on our $10 note.

HOLT

It's nice that we remember Harold Holt with a suburb, because some of his colleagues were pretty quick to move on.

'Channel 7 in Melbourne asked me to appear on the 7 pm news to pay a tribute to the missing PM,' said former Liberal MP Don Chipp of the day the prime minister disappeared in the surf at Cheviot Beach. 'I was a very junior minister – number 25 in a pecking order of 27. I said that surely there would be more senior ministers or officials available, but I was wrong. The grab for the coveted prize of prime minister had already begun. Votes were being marshalled, contenders were already on the phone . . . HSV7 found no-one else willing to appear.'

HUGHES

Australia's seventh prime minister and longest-serving MP, Billy Hughes was a man you could rely on.

But it probably wasn't very advisable. Hughes represented four different electorates over the course of a 51-year career in parliament, and changed parties no less than five times. 'Billy, you are the "googly bowler" of Australian politics,' someone once said to him, 'but why is it that you have been in almost every party in Australia except the Nationals?'

'Good God, man,' Hughes indignantly replied, 'you have to draw the line somewhere!'

LAKE BURLEY GRIFFIN

A central part of Walter Burley Griffin's 'ideal city', this big artificial lake in the centre of Canberra was built long after his death.

This was a pity in more ways than one. For one thing, the architect never got to see it. And for another, he wasn't in a position to point out that 'Burley' was actually his *middle* name.

MANUKA

A 'manuka' is a type of tree only found in New Zealand, so what's it doing in our nation's capital?

Well, as undesirable as the idea may seem, the Australian Constitution still includes a provision which would let New Zealand hop on board as our seventh state. The suburb of Manuka was named in 1912, in an effort to sweeten the deal.

MONARO RANGE

According to Olaf Ruhen, a man who may need a girlfriend, the meaning of Monaro is 'most probably "breast", for the hills, particularly towards the southern end, are breast-shaped and have outcrops of granite for nipples at their peaks.'

MOUNT TENNANT

Mount Tennant and Mount Ainslie are not very close and neither were Tennant and Ainslie.

The hills get their names from a wealthy ACT farmer called James Ainslie, and the unusually thorough bushranger who burgled his home. Not content with finding a handful of coins, John Tennant also made off with a handkerchief, three red shirts, a pair of trousers and a small sack of flour.

O'MALLEY

A US-born insurance salesman who got around in a Stetson (together with a gold fob watch and diamond tie clip), King O'Malley somehow ended his life as a prominent Labor MP. Chiefly remembered for taking the 'u' out of 'Labor', and doing his best to ban all alcohol, he helped to manage parliament's move to Canberra in 1913, and was rewarded with the name of a suburb.

Fair enough, I suppose, so long as we overlook what this 'founding father' actually thought.

'Surely honourable members are satisfied with the present home of the Parliament,' he argued in 1909, in response to the suggestion that honourable members leave Melbourne. 'Surely we have every comfort which Christian men could have in a Christian land? Why should we leave a healthy, prosperous, successful city like Melbourne, where the rents are low, and the people are healthy and intelligent, and where we have libraries, great newspapers and the best of society?'

Canberra could be good, though, surely?

No. 'This is . . . a district which . . . is so dry that a crow desiring to put in a weekend vacation there would have to carry its water-bag. I do not wish to see the capital established in such an undesirable place.'

REID

Australians like their leaders lean, probably because it is thought to denote energy or discipline.

How things have changed. Prime minister in 1904 and '05, and now the name of a suburb, Sir George Reid was roughly the size of three prime ministers, having been 'reared on porridge and treacle'. Famous for always falling asleep in parliament – and for once asking the Prince of Wales and Archbishop of Canterbury to please make sure that he stayed awake during a speech – Sir George was as witty as he was fleshy, which meant that he was witty indeed.

'What are you going to call it, George?' a heckler once yelled, in reference to his protruding tum. His response? 'If it's a boy, I'll call it after myself and if it's a girl I'll call it Victoria. But if, as I strongly suspect, it's nothing but piss and wind, I'll name it after you.'

WHITLAM

Currently under construction, the new suburb of Whitlam will be named after one of our most iconic prime ministers. Plans for it weren't announced until after he died, but that's okay, his self-esteem was healthy enough.

'You can be sure of one thing,' Gough once said when someone asked him how he planned to greet God in heaven. 'I shall treat him as an equal.'

A Note on Sources

The majority of place names were researched through the following sources:

Appleton, R and B, *The Cambridge Dictionary of Australian Place Names*, Cambridge University Press, Melbourne, 1992

Beatty, B, 'There's Drama & Tragedy In Place Names', *Sydney Morning Herald*, 2 August 1947

Boardman, A and Harvey, R, *Great Events in Australia's History*, Five Mile Press, Melbourne, 1985

Cockburn, R, *What's in a Name? A Nomenclature of South Australia*, Ferguson, Adelaide, 1984

Corbett, C, 'Putting Australia on the Map: "Mapping Our World" at the National Library of Australia', *Monthly*, February 2014

Flinders, M, *A Voyage to Terra Australis*, G and W Nicol, London, 1814

Giles, E, *Australia Twice Traversed*, University of Adelaide, 2004
http://webdoc.sub.gwdg.de/ebook/p/2005/adelaide/etext.library.adelaide.edu.au/g/giles/ernest/g47a/

Haynes, J, *The Best Australian Yarns and Other True Stories*, Allen & Unwin, Sydney, 2013

Hunt, D, *Girt: The Unauthorised History of Australia*, Black Inc, Melbourne, 2013

Kennedy, B and B, *Australian Place Names*, Hodder & Stoughton, Sydney, 1988

King, J, *A Cartoon History of Australia*, Savvas, Adelaide, 1983

Lau, M and Stehr, E, *Revised and Interesting Place Names and History of Australia*, Scribd.com

MacCallum, M, *Australian Political Anecdotes*, Oxford University Press, Melbourne, 1994

Martin, A, *One Thousand and More Place Names in New South Wales*, NSW Bookstall Co., Sydney, 1943

Martin, A, *One Thousand and More Place Names in Queensland, New Zealand and the Pacific*, NSW Bookstall Co., Sydney, 1944

Nicholson, M, *The Little Aussie Fact Book*, Penguin, Melbourne, 1998

Pearson, M, *Great Southern Land: The Maritime Exploration of Terra Australis*, Australian Government Department of the Environment and Heritage, Canberra, 2005

Pepworth, B, *Historic Places of Australia*, Macmillan, Melbourne, 1981

Reed, AW, *Aboriginal Words and Place Names*, Rigby, Adelaide, 1976

Reed, AW, *Place Names of Australia*, Reed, Sydney, 1973

Ridley, B and B, *Ozzobooko: Australian Place Names Revisited*, Inca Books, Perth, 1988

Robson, P, *Yorkey's Knob: Weird and Wonderful Australian Place Names*, Random House, Sydney, 2007

Ross, J (ed.), *Chronicle of Australia*, Penguin, Melbourne, 1993

Taylor, P, *Australian Ripping Yarns*, Five Mile Press, Melbourne, 2004

Taylor, P, *Australian Ripping Yarns II*, Five Mile Press, Melbourne, 2005

Tindale, NB, *Aboriginal Tribes of Australia,* ANU Press, Canberra, 1974

Wajnryb, R, *Australian Place Name Stories*, Lothian Books, Melbourne, 2006

Other individual entries were researched through these sources:

ADELAIDE

'His Most Gracious Majesty King William the IV', The British Museum Online Collection

    http://www.britishmuseum.org/research/collection_online/collection_object_details.aspx?objectId=3532123&partId=1&people=153952&peoA=-153952-2-70&sortBy=producerSort&page=1

ALICE SPRINGS

Grainger, EE, 'A Woman Like Alice', *Sydney Morning Herald*, 3 May 1952

    https://news.google.com/newspapers?nid=1301&dat=19520503&id=S-dJVAAAAIBAJ&sjid=IsQDAAAAIBAJ&pg=7057,208264&hl=en

ALLIGATOR GORGE

'Place Names of South Australia – A', State Library of South Australia

    http://www.slsa.sa.gov.au/manning/pn/a/a6.htm

ANKATELL

'Thomas Peel 1793–1865', *Western Australia Now and Then*

    http://www.wanowandthen.com/Thomas-Peel.html

A NOTE ON SOURCES

ARAMAC
Joyce, RB, 'Mackenzie, Sir Robert Ramsay (1811–1873)', *Australian Dictionary of Biography*, Melbourne University Press, 1974
http://adb.anu.edu.au/biography/mackenzie-sir-robert-ramsay-4109

ARANA HILLS
Potter, R, 'Place Name Origins A to G', Piula Publications.
http://www.piulapublications.com/?page_id=3782

AUSTRALIA/EARLY USES OF THE TERM 'AUSTRALIA'
Clarke, P, 'Putting Australia on the Map', *The Conversation*, 11 August 2014
http://theconversation.com/putting-australia-on-the-map-29816

AUSTRALIA/TERRA WHO-THE-HELL-KNOWS? (500 – 1606)
'Who Did Discover Australia? The Muslims', The Discovery and Exploration of Australia.
http://www.australiaforeveryone.com.au/discovery/muslims.htm

AUSTRALIAN CAPITAL TERRITORY
'The Australian Capital Territory – Canberra: Fifty Years of Development', Australian Bureau of Statistics, 2012
http://www.abs.gov.au/Ausstats/abs@.nsf/0/
d41f48b6cb4d1240ca2569de00281139?OpenDocument

BADGER HEAD
'Charlotte Badger (1778–?)', *Rejected Princesses*
http://www.rejectedprincesses.com/princesses/charlotte-badger

BARNEY POINT
'Barney, George (1792–1862)', *Australian Dictionary of Biography* online
http://adb.anu.edu.au/biography/barney-george-1744

BOOBYALLA
'Boobyalla', *Merrian-Webster Dictonary* online
http://www.merriam-webster.com/dictionary/boobyalla

BRISBANE
Heydon, JD, 'Brisbane, Sir Thomas Makdougall (1773–1860)', *Australian Dictionary of Biography* online
http://adb.anu.edu.au/biography/brisbane-sir-thomas-makdougall-1827

CADELL
'Francis Cadell (explorer)', Wikipedia: The Free Encyclopaedia (Wikimedia Foundation Inc., updated 12 April 2016, at 05:37.)
https://en.wikipedia.org/wiki/Francis_Cadell_(explorer)

CANNIBAL CREEK

'The Old Telegraph Track', Cape York Travel Guide
    http://www.cape-york-australia.com/old-telegraph-track.html

CARLTON

Huish, R, 'Memoirs of George the Fourth: Descriptive of the Most Interesting
Scenes of His Private and Public Life, and the Important Events of His Memorable
Reign: with Characteristic Sketches of All the Celebrated Men who Were His
Friends and Companions as a Prince, and His Ministers and Friends as a Monarch:
Comp. from Authentic Sources, and Documents in the King's Library in the British
Museum, &c', Adams, Victor and Company, New York, 1830, p 257

COLLINGWOOD

Lloyd, C, 'The British Seaman 1200-1860: A Social Survey', Associated University
Presses, New Jersey, 1970, p 210

DARWIN

'Place names register extract: Holmes', Northern Territory Place Names Register
    http://www.ntlis.nt.gov.au/placenames/view.jsp?id=22296

DEAD MANS GULLY

O'Reilly, A, 'Dead Man's Gully, Darnum', Odd History Australia
    http://www.oddhistory.com.au/gippsland/dead-mans-gully-darnum/

DEAD MANS PASS

'Deadman's Pass', Gawler Public Library
    http://www.gawler.sa.gov.au/webdata/resources/files/Dead_man_s_pass.pdf

DENILIQUIN

'Deniliquin', *Sydney Morning Herald*, 8 February 2004
    http://www.smh.com.au/news/New-South-Wales/
    Deniliquin/2005/02/17/1108500193478.html

DEVILS GARDENS RESERVE

'Place Names of South Australia – D', State Library of South Australia
    http://www.slsa.sa.gov.au/manning/pn/d/d3.htm

DUNTROON

Tim the Yowie Man, 'Canberra's spooks not just confined to ASIO: the ACT's
"haunted houses"', *Canberra Times*, 2 March 2015
    http://www.canberratimes.com.au/act-news/canberra-life/canberras-spooks-
    not-just-confined-to-asio-the-acts-haunted-houses-20150226-13q42o.html

FRASER ISLAND

Brown, E, 'Eliza Anne Fraser', *Australian Dictionary of Biography* online
    http://adb.anu.edu.au/biography/fraser-eliza-anne-12929

FLINDERS RANGES

'Trim', Monument Australia
http://monumentaustralia.org.au/themes/landscape/discovery/
display/51873-trim

GENTLE ANNIE

'Black Annis, Leicestershire', *Mysterious Britain and Ireland: mysteries, legends and the paranormal*
http://www.mysteriousbritain.co.uk/forums/mysterious-britain/folklore-and-legends/black-annis-leicestershire.html

GINS LEAP

Richards, D, 'The Last Words of Xavier Herbert', *National Times*, 18 to 24 January 1985

GLUEPOT RESERVE

'Place Names of South Australia – G', State Library of South Australia
http://www.slsa.sa.gov.au/manning/pn/g/g6.htm

HELLS GATES

Collins, P, 'A Journey through hell's gate', *The Age*, 29 October 2002
http://www.theage.com.au/articles/2002/10/28/1035683357802.html

HERVEY BAY

'The Exhausting Naval Adventures of Augustus Hervey', Rogues Gallery, 10 December 2013
http://www.roguesgalleryonline.com/
all-aborad-the-exhausting-naval-adventures-of-augustus-hervey/

HOPE VALLEY

'Place Names of South Australia – H', State Library of South Australia
http://www.slsa.sa.gov.au/digitalpubs/placenamesofsouthaustralia/H.pdf
'Adelaide: Adelaide City', State Library of South Australia
http://www.slsa.sa.gov.au/manning/adelaide/adelaide/adelaide.htm

HUMPTY DOO

'Humpty Doo: small town between Darwin and Kakadu', *Sydney Morning Herald*, 8 February 2004
http://www.smh.com.au/news/northern-territory/humpty-doo/2005/02/17/1108500201628.html

KING GEORGE SOUND

Kelly, D, 'The Complicated Madness of King George III', KnowledgeNuts, 4 April 2014
http://knowledgenuts.com/2014/04/04/
the-complicated-madness-of-king-george-iii/

LOGAN CREEK

'Ghosts of Queensland Brisbane and the Brisbane Region', QueenslandHistory.com
> http://www.chapelhill.homeip.net/FamilyHistory/Other/QueenslandHistory/
> TheGhostsofQueensland.htm

MACKSVILLE

Irish, CA, Names of Railway Stations in New South Wales with their Meaning and Origin
> http://www.nswrail.net/library/station_names.php

MARYLANDS

'Place Names of South-East Queensland, Australia'
> http://www.chapelhill.homeip.net/horton/copies/piula_Placenames/page42.
> html

MELBOURNE

'The queen, her prime minister, and the kissing of hands . . .', The Virtual Victorian, May, 2010.
> http://virtualvictorian.blogspot.com.au/2010/05/queenher-prime-
> minister-and-kissing-of.html

MEMORY COVE

'Investigator: HMS, Cutter', ABC's Shipwrecks
> http://www.abc.net.au/backyard/shipwrecks/sa/catastrophe.htm

MIEPOLL

Beatty, B, *A Treasury of Australian Folk Tales and Traditions*, Ure Smith, Sydney, 1968

MONSTER CREEK

Tasmanian Museum and Art Gallery, 'West Coast Sea Monster', Shaping Tasmania
> http://shapingtasmania.tmag.tas.gov.au/object.aspx?ID=32

MOOBALL

'Mooball', Australian Explorer
> https://www.australianexplorer.com/mooball.htm

MOUNT BABBAGE

'Place Names of South Australia – B', State Library of South Australia
> http://www.slsa.sa.gov.au/manning/pn/b/b1.htm

MOUNT COOLUM

Sunshine Coast Libraries, 'Local Indigenous Heritage'
> https://library.sunshinecoast.qld.gov.au/library/documents/heritage/black_
> swan_indigenous_sign.pdf

MOUNT HORROCKS

Flinders Ranges, 'The Explorers'
http://history.flindersranges.com.au/discovery/explorers/

MOUNT HORROR

Billings, P, 'On watch: a tower calling', *The Examiner*, 19 January 2014
http://www.examiner.com.au/story/2032843/on-watch-a-tower-calling/

MUCKADILLA

Tilma, L, 'Thirsty for more?', *Outback Queensland*, 15 October 2015
http://www.outbackqueensland.com.au/news/thirsty-for-more/

NEW SOUTH WALES

Welsh, G, 'What's in a place name?', Anzlic Committee on Surveying and
Mapping, December 2001
http://www.icsm.gov.au/cgna/lesson/story01.html

NORTHAMPTON

'John Stephen Hampton 1862–1868', The Constitutional Centre of Western
Australia
https://www.constitutionalcentre.wa.gov.au/ExhibitionsOnline/
GovernorsAndPremiers/Governors/Pages/Hampton.aspx

PEMULWUY

'Pemulwuy: A War of Two Laws Part 1', Transcript of ABC's *Message Stick,* 9 May
2010
http://www.abc.net.au/tv/messagestick/stories/s2893382.htm

PINKY FLAT

'Place Names of South Australia – P', State Library of South Australia
http://www.slsa.sa.gov.au/manning/pn/p/p6.htm

POINT PIPER

'The Inglorious John Piper', Unearth the Rocks
http://unearth.therocks.com/explore/100-george-st/the-inglorious-john-piper/

POISONED WATERHOLE CREEK

Taylor, C, 'Memory of massacres "should be kept alive"', *Daily Advertiser*, 1 July 2013
http://www.dailyadvertiser.com.au/story/1607221/
memory-of-massacres-should-be-kept-alive/

PORT DAVEY

Eldershaw, PR, 'Thomas Davey', *Australian Dictionary of Biography* online
http://adb.anu.edu.au/biography/davey-thomas-1959

PORT HACKING

Walsh, GP, 'Henry Hacking', *Australian Dictionary of Biography* online
http://adb.anu.edu.au/biography/hacking-henry-2140

PRETTY SALLY HILL

Thom, G, 'What Happened to Pretty Sally?' Kilmore Historical Society,
3 September 2015
https://kilmorehistory.wordpress.com/2015/09/03/
what-happened-to-pretty-sally/

PUTTY

'Putty', Wikipedia: The Free Encyclopaedia (Wikimedia Foundation Inc., updated
19 June 2016, at 19:44.)
https://en.wikipedia.org/wiki/Putty

QUEENSLAND

'How Queensland got its name', *Courier-Mail* online

REPENTANCE CREEK

'Repentance Creek', Ancestry.com
http://freepages.genealogy.rootsweb.ancestry.com/~hcastle/transcripts/kathy_
pearson/transcripts/repentancecreek.html

RESTORATION ISLAND

'Norfolk Island Under Siege', Facebook
https://www.facebook.com/norfolkislandundersiege/photos/
pb.1091421597567222.-2207520000.1463446067./ 1108973642478684/?type=
3&theater

SEA LAKE

'Sea lake', Wikipedia: The Free Encyclopaedia (Wikimedia Foundation Inc., updated
29 June 2016, at 10:49.)
https://en.wikipedia.org/wiki/Sea_Lake

SOUTH AUSTRALIA

'Flinders Ranges Research: Pieter Nuyts', South Australian History
http://www.southaustralianhistory.com.au/index.html
'Dutch Colonial Governors and Administrators', Booksllc.net (Excerpt original
taken from 'Pieter Nuyts', Wikipedia: The Free Encyclopaedia (Wikimedia
Foundation Inc., updated 10 July 2016, at 16:28.)
http://www.booksllc.net/book.cfm?id=3617295

SYDNEY

'Thomas Townshend, Lord Viscount Sydney', National Portrait Gallery
http://www.portrait.gov.au/people/-viscount-sydney-1733
Clark, M, *A History of Australia*, Volume 1, Melbourne University Press, 1995

A NOTE ON SOURCES

TRIAL HARBOUR
Eaves, R, 'Trial Harbour ladies love the extremes', ABC Northern Tasmania, 14 May 2014
> http://www.abc.net.au/local/photos/2014/05/14/4004576.htm

TROUSERS POINT
Danger, C and Bishop, W, 'Top 10 anchorages to visit in Tasmania's Furneaux Group', My Sailing, 30 July 2015
> http://www.mysailing.com.au/news/
> top-10-anchorages-to-visit-in-tasmania-s-furneaux-group

VICTORIA
Clarke, ID, 'Indigenous and Minority Placenames', The Australian National University Press, Canberra 1958, p 230

WARREN
'Warren: quiet township on the Macquarie River', *Sydney Morning Herald* 8 February 2004
> http://www.smh.com.au/news/new-south-wales/
> warren/2005/02/17/1108500200060.html

WESTERN AUSTRALIA
Tent, J, in 'Four Million Place Names And Counting', newmatilda.com, 25 April 2010
> https://newmatilda.com/2010/04/25/four-million-place-names-and-counting/

WISEMANS FERRY
Sandra, 'Know your history – Wiseman's Ferry', *Kuringai Examiner*, 29 July 2014
> http://www.kgex.com.au/know-history-wisemans-ferry/

WOODBINE
'Woodbine, New South Wales', Wikipedia
> https://en.wikipedia.org/wiki/Woodbine,_New_South_Wales

YORKEYS KNOB
Adams, P, 'Rooty Hill meets Titty Bong', *The Australian*, 13 January 2007
> http://www.theaustralian.com.au/archive/news/rooty-hill-meets-titty-bong/
> story-e6frg6rf-1111112830989

ZUYTDORP CLIFFS
'Wreck of the Zuytdorp', Western Australian Museum
> http://museum.wa.gov.au/explore/videos/wreck-zuytdorp

hachette
AUSTRALIA

If you would like to find out more about Hachette Australia, our authors, upcoming events and new releases you can visit our website, Facebook or follow us on Twitter:

hachette.com.au
facebook.com/HachetteAustralia
twitter.com/HachetteAus

eamonevans.com.au